Preventing Shrink: Life in Loss Prevention
By Alan Hoekman

First Printing, 2015

ISBN 978-1-511417-64-8

Email questions or comments to Alan.Hoekman@gmail.com

www.AlanHoekman.com

Preventing Shrink: Life in Loss Prevention

"So I'm watching this guy right in front of me take a can of cat food off the shelf, walk to the kitchen accessory aisle, and grab a can opener. He then uses the can opener to open the cat food, and with a spoon he already had concealed into his pocket, he starts eating it right in the store. I had never stopped anyone for stealing or for eating cat food, so I was a little excited—until the store manager told me to wait for the police." I was telling my buddy about a recent apprehension that I had just made at work.

"Why didn't the store manager want you to just take him yourself?" he questioned, seeming a little intrigued.

"Well, this jerk was wearing a backpack with God-knows-what inside, but the backpack was only halfway covering the two katana-looking swords that he had strapped to his back. Now I know I'm not invincible, but I figured it would take him longer to get one of the swords out than it would take me to take him to the ground. Besides, I was not about to let some Teenage Mutant Ninja Turtle wannabe steal my damn cat food; well, the store's food anyway."

At this moment, I could tell that my friend had decided in his head that I was only going on about some "big fish" story that couldn't actually have happened. I was used to it when I talked about my work to people that didn't understand the business. So many times in the middle of a story, my audience just turns off and stops believing in the story. I get it though: Who could believe that some guy with katana swords was eating stolen cat food in the middle of a store? So early in my career, and I had already made it a point not to talk about work to anyone that didn't actively request to know more about my day. This story in particular started because my friend saw a swarm of police cars at my work a few days ago and wanted to know why.

I was never fond of people thinking that I was lying, so I'd started to clip out newspaper articles about stories that had happened to me— that way I could feel a little more vindicated when I felt my friends losing interest in what they thought could only be a fallacy. I slid the newspaper article to my friend as he was sipping his beer; he instantly did a double-take at the headline before he began to read the clip. After a slight pause to read the article, he took another sip of his beer and then turned to me, "You stopped some crazy SOB with swords over some cat food?"

I see now how it must have sounded crazy to someone on the outside looking in, but it didn't really matter what a person stole. If they took something that didn't belong to them inside of my store, I would stop them no matter what. Maybe it's that fact that I was ex-army, or maybe I had some instilled knowledge of right and wrong, or more possibly maybe it was the license to fight someone doing something wrong that attracted me to the job; either way, I was hooked on Loss Prevention.

Contents

What is Loss Prevention?

Anyone who has ever worked retail will tell you that, when they started, they were told about a scary guy that kept to himself whose only job was to catch you doing something wrong. This is not the truth at all about loss prevention—well, at least not the full truth. Being in loss prevention, your job is pretty basic: stop losses from happening inside of the store. Now, that means stopping shoplifters, finding paperwork issues, and yes, sometimes it means talking to associates that may be creating a loss (this could, however, create a fun interrogation moment—but more on that later). The point is, most loss prevention guys don't really care if you are parked in a handicapped spot or if you smoke on the wrong side of the parking lot—but yes, we will be the first to know about it. Hell, I'll be honest; I have smoked in an undesignated spot in every place that I have worked at while doing loss prevention, and a lot of times it was with the store manager. In fact, some of my fondest memories are smoking with a store manager on the roof of the building, or smoking with another that would swear up and down to everyone else that they had never smoked. Don't get me wrong, rules are in place to keep a business moving forward without issue; however, a loss prevention member's role is not to write you up if you don't say "bless you" when someone sneezes. The scary bad guy persona is just to help us keep a distance, because we can see things more clearly from the sidelines than we can from the middle of the game.

Shoplifting Theft (Externals):

It seems as though shoplifters are the main thing that stop new loss prevention recruits from joining the ranks; they are, of course, most retail chains' archnemeses. Shoplifters are a huge cause of stores losing money every year, and this results in stores having to combat it by increasing their prices for what merchandise is left. It goes without saying that this is where store managers like to blame most of their store's problems. You lost 3% of your merchandise this year, store manager, "Because of shoplifters." You don't have any merchandise on the sales floor, store manager, "Because shoplifters stole it all." None of your employees showed up to work today, store manager, "Because they are scared of the shoplifters." You yourself showed up late to work today, store manager, "Because I was chasing a shoplifter."

While shoplifters do in fact play a large role in stores' losing money, it doesn't even equate to half of the average store's shrink (loss). The truth is that, going into loss prevention, you have to know that your job will be scrutinized whenever the store is doing poorly. I remember one position in particular where I worked 70 hours a week on average for a year straight. My numbers were astronomically higher than any of my predecessors; however, at the end of the year, when the store was doing poorly, they flew in multiple teams to question my performance. What a shot to the ego that was, after having a closet full of awards from everywhere that I had been, including that same store.

I personally categorize shoplifters into four main groups: those that want, those that sell, those that have habit, and those that need. Those that want are usually the easiest to catch, and are the ones that steal from your store on a daily basis. They are typically younger kids who know that their parents are not going to buy them a candy bar or a video game if they ask them. These types of shoplifters are very compliant most of the time, and do not give you much trouble. The real trouble comes when the parent leaves work and comes to get the kid from your office. See, the parents are going to be mad, maybe even livid, and they sometimes don't know exactly where to place the blame. To yell at their kid would mean that they may have done something wrong while raising their child, so yelling at the mean guy that stopped their kid is sometimes much easier. On countless occasions, I have had parents come into my office after their kid was stopped for stealing, and begin to accuse me of planting the items on them, watching them because I was racist (even if I was the same race), or wasting their time because a CD only cost a few dollars versus the time they are losing at work to come down. I have been yelled at, cursed, threatened, and even pushed by parents looking for a scapegoat. I have never taken it personally, but I knew that I would see that kid back again in my office very soon.

The next type of shoplifter is the one that makes a living doing it. They are the ones that come in and steal high-priced items so that they can sell the items later on. These types of shoplifters are usually the most experienced and sometimes most dangerous. They will use theft devices so that they can be more proficient at their crimes and will undoubtedly be ready for you when you try and stop them. Sometimes their theft devices or tools will be common, like a normal backpack that they fill with multiple Levis (yes, jeans, stores sell them for $75 and criminals sell them for $30 on the street), and sometimes their tools may be so intricate that you don't even believe what they are doing until it is too late. I have seen a girl who looked pregnant when it was just a hollowed-out container used to hide merchandise. I have seen a man with a five-liner jacket (one jacket, five different liners) so that he could hide multiple jewelry pieces throughout each hidden compartment, magnets to take off sensors, aluminum-foil-wrapped purses to get through sensors; the list could go on for hours.

The good shoplifters will work in groups so that one is always looking for you. This becomes a problem when you typically work by yourself. The main thing that you must do is watch your surroundings so that the "lookout" doesn't sneak up behind you. One of the scariest moments in my career was when I was about to stop a girl from stealing hundreds of dollars of makeup. It seemed like a basic shoplifter, but as we were both going for the front door I noticed a man walk into the store at that same moment. The man had his hands in his pockets and was scanning everyone leaving the store—everyone except the shoplifter, who was looking down when he came in. I was just about to grab the girl when the guy walked behind me. I turned around, letting the shoplifter go, just in time to see Crocodile Dundee's knife inches away from my stomach. The man was the shoplifter's lookout and was waiting for someone to stop her. I pushed his arm with the knife away and he stumbled toward the door. The female shoplifter hadn't left the store and tried to help him gain his balance. The knife went through her like she was warm butter. Later it was found out that she was pregnant; the baby didn't make it, but she did. I know I may seem a bit callous, but the knife was intended for me and I am still just happy that some poor customer did not get the brunt end of the knife. The rule that will keep a good loss prevention person in his job the longest is: never let your guard down. If you stop paying attention to your surroundings because you feel complacent, that's the time you will get hurt. While I do still feel bad for that shoplifter, I did get to go home to my family that night.

The next category of shoplifter is the one that does it on habit. They are the shoplifters that feel the urge to steal whenever they are in a store. Sometimes they will swear to you that they didn't even know they stole; it is just an ongoing battle that they have with themselves. This type of shoplifter usually steals the weirdest things in a store. I once saw a lady who opened up a bag of cotton balls, removed one, which she placed in her pocket, and leave. I didn't stop her that day, but a week later she came back and stole a screw off of the water fountain. She actually spent the time to use her personal screwdriver and slowly remove the tiny screw. Instead of stopping her, I told the store manager about the lady. My laughter must have been unsettling to them as I told the story, because they were not very amused. The next time the lady came in, she was with a rather large guy. I will secretly admit to you now something that I have never admitted while doing the job before. Depending on my mood, sometimes knowing that I was about to go up against a large guy excited me for the challenge, and sometimes it made me wonder why in the hell I would really pick this occupation; either way, I always went and hoped for the best. While the lady was in the store this time, she waited until the man was away before she began her game. As soon as he walked to a different part of the store, she began taking clothing off of hangers and then concealing the hangers inside of her jacket. I waited for her to leave the store and then stopped her for the hangers. Luckily for me, the guy she was with just shook his head and left her as he walked outside. Once inside my office, she began to cry and asked me to call her parole officer and her therapist. Apparently, the recent treatment for her kleptomania was to go to the park and train her brain into thinking that stealing leaves was the same thing as merchandise. When her house was filled up with so many leaves, to the point that guests had nowhere to sit, she decided to go back to the stores. Although she requested that I press charges on her, I could not see myself going to court for a 65-year-old lady stealing two hangers, a screw, and a cotton ball. FYI, if you are missing a screw to your water fountain, she is probably still at large (code name: White Betty).

The last category of shoplifter, and the hardest for me, is the one that does it out of need. Now, you will never convince me that you need the newest Blu-Ray out there because "it's my fave," nor will I blink twice when you tell me that you cannot live without makeup because "I have a date tonight with a hottie," and there is no way that I will care when you say that you stole a pillow because "I have a really hard time sleeping," because trust me: I have heard them all before (wait until you read the section on excuses); but the shoplifters that bother me are the ones that steal lunch meat and eat as much of it as they can before you stop them. To be good at loss prevention, you really have to have tough skin, but times like these when I could feel my heart sink, I wished I could do something more. Although these people were stealing and committing a crime, I couldn't help but feel as though I were in the movie Demolition Man and going after the people from the sewers that were just trying to survive. Yes, it was my Achilles' heel. My wife finally gave me the idea to keep a list of resources that could help people like this. This list had everything from places that handed out food, to shelters, to clothing banks. I still had to stop these people, and at times I was even known to buy them a meal while we waited for the police to run their names—but I felt slightly better when I could show them that there were resources out there that they might not have tried yet. I could always tell the ones that really needed the list; they would instantly start to read and thumb through it, sometimes asking me if they could use my phone to call a few. One day there was a boy (I believe he was 13) who was stealing some food. I don't remember exactly what the food was, but it was just enough for him to eat at the moment. He was very apologetic, but you could tell that he knew a level of hunger that I had never known. While talking to him in my office, he took off one of his shirts because it was hot (by the way, loss prevention offices rarely have heaters or air conditioners; thanks a lot whoever thought we would be fine without them). As he took off the shirt, he pulled his undershirt up a little and I could see his stomach. I do not think I could describe to you exactly what the sight was, other than his stomach and his back seem to be one. Right under this poor boy's rib cage, his body was concaved into itself, showing a sight that you should only see in a third-world country where food was scarce. It was clear that this boy had not eaten in quite some time. I don't remember if it was me or one of the other managers in the room that went to get the boy food, but when we gave it to him, he held on as tight as if it were the first time he had seen food in his life. The boy began to tell me of countless foster homes and boys' homes that he had run away from—sometimes leaving because he was beat up and sometimes because of much worse crimes that had been committed against him. For the past week, he had been living in a drainage pipe about a mile away from the store, hoping not to be found, only venturing out when he was feeling brave. As the police began to run his name, I had already informed my wife. Being the most supportive wife in the world, she started to make plans for the newest member of our family. Sadly, the last two foster homes that he had been in had still not reported him missing, but unfortunately for him, one of the boys' homes had placed a missing-persons report for him over a year ago and he was returned. I can't give much advice as to this type of shoplifter, as they have caused me the most amount of grief, but what I can say is to treat people with respect even when they are committing a crime. You might not have a clue as to what they are going through that made them choose the action they did.

Paperwork Shrink:

Oh, the joys of reading countless stacks of reports just to find that the computer generated a price error and a $100 microwave is showing at the registers as a $10 microwave. While this is absolutely a problem that needs to be addressed quickly, this will never be my favorite type of work in loss prevention. Some companies will put all of their "auditing" work on the loss prevention person because they just don't want to have someone else do it. I do understand that the loss prevention person should have their hands in everything to make sure that everyone is being honest— but let's face it, a guy that tackles shoplifters will never have the same amount of enthusiasm about reading stacks of papers that have been printed in old DOS typeface. There is also the problem that auditing paperwork is a full-time job, so when you give those same papers to someone with multiple other challenges, there is a good chance that they will not be able to do it all without skimming a little. The best way to truly get an actual audit done from within the store is to have a district auditor that will spend their time going through all of the stores in a market and give a once-over. This will allow someone to be dedicated to the paperwork who knows exactly what they are looking at. Besides, when they see a problem in one store, chances are it is happening in another one, saving the auditor time.

Unfortunately, when stores downsize, they start to take away multiple positions throughout the company, and the auditor may be one of the positions to be cut within a store. This is definitely sad for the loss prevention person, who has to pick up the slack, and for the company that ends up losing hundreds of thousands of dollars because no one ever finds the mistakes. I know it may seem crazy to think that paperwork issues can amount to so much; however, it is normal to find a markdown mistake that has cost a store a few thousand, a billing issue that has cost a few thousand, a shipping issue that has cost a few thousand, and so many others. By the time you add up, in just one store, the amount that you could find, it would be enough for a great salary for a few people to work throughout the year. So why do companies not all have this position? All I can say is this: I started, organized, and ran an audit team throughout one company (while doing loss prevention). My team was finding $20,000-$100,000 during each audit of a new store that we went through, to the point that we were actually asked to go to different states and continue on with our audit. After about a year, the company said, "great job, the stores should be able to take it from here." Now, this is a great hope that the company had, except for one small problem: retention of employees sucks in retail. By the time my team would audit the same store after a six-month follow up, the old employees that we had trained were gone. This meant that my team had to retrain a new bunch of people on how to do the job correctly. So, if there are any company big wigs out there, get an audit team: It will save you tons of money.

Since I have already expressed my lack of love for paperwork, I will tell you that there is always a way to make your paperwork more efficient. Through the many companies that I have worked, I have found several amazing tools and systems that were very beneficial when doing paperwork. At one store, they had a system set up for tracking when a register was over or short, and which cashiers had been on it. Before that store, I had never seen a system like it, nor have I again. So when I moved on to a new company, I made a system like it and used it with great success. Two different companies loved the idea so much that it went company-wide. Now, let me assure you that there are people much smarter than I out there who could have made a better program by using hundreds of different formulas on Excel to get the same results, but they didn't. Another company had a program for checking refunds and markdowns to insure that they were not losing money in those ways. Again, these programs did not exist in any other company that I had been to, and would have saved said other companies thousands of dollars. So, if there is a company out there that really wants to reduce their shrink and be able to lower the price of their goods to the American consumer, I would suggest partnering with other retailers to ensure you have the proper tools to capture where you are losing money. If you don't know where to start, just see what other companies are struggling with and what they are the leaders of, and learn from them. One of my favorite quotes comes from Sam Walton, founder of Walmart, who said: "When it comes to good ideas, steal shamelessly." If you can win at the back of house operations, then you will recover at least 15% of your shrink. While you may not be the CEO of a company, it is still a good idea to converse with others in your area at different retail stores to make sure you are using the most up-to-date equipment or tools; I have done this everywhere that I have been employed and it works amazingly. Other loss prevention people will normally great you with open arms and be happy to show you what they are doing, which will help you with your own job. If the loss prevention person doesn't seem to be the most knowledgeable, then the back-of-house people are probably doing the majority of the work and can still help. I partnered with one cash office lady from a different retail store because they were amazing at finding register mistakes. She opened my eyes to a new way of looking at the errors and how to spot them. In return, I gave her the program that I made for finding over/shortage problems, and she almost cried. We both had amazing results that year at our different retailers. Just remember, partnering with the "enemy" does not have to be a bad thing—it could lead to both companies getting a better handle on their own revenue.

Employee Theft (Internals):

Employee theft is actually the number one cause of loss across almost all retailers. While the amounts of their theft may seem small by comparison, a normal employee that steals will continue to do so until they are caught or until they leave the business. There are a great many ways that employees steal, such as taking merchandise that they didn't pay for, giving unnecessary discounts to friends and family, taking money from the register (till tapping), not ringing up all items while checking someone out (sweet-hearting), helping shoplifters, taking excessive breaks, time card abuse, etc. Notice how I did not say smoking in an undesignated area or parking in a handicapped space. As I have gone to different retailers, I have found that different companies place different weight on these crimes. While each one is against the policy of every company I have been to, only some fire employees for committing them. If you ask me, if you are costing the company more money than you are worth, then I believe that you should be fired. I will say that on some occasions I have found that improper training was the reason an employee got sent to my office, and corrective action was the only thing that needed to be done to fix the problem; however, if the problem persists after additional training, then I would personally walk them to the door.

Going back to companies placing different weight on these misbehaviors, I have been to a few stores that did not feel as though giving your associate discount card to random friends and customers was worth firing over. In these same stores, I have seen thousands of dollars lost because of an additional discount that was given to people that didn't work at that particular establishment. There are two problems with this: First, retail employees don't normally make a lot, so the fact that their company gives them a discount to continue to shop there is a big bonus for them; let them have it. The main problem for the companies is that they did not intend for everyone to get that discount on their merchandise, nor can they afford for all of their customers to get such discounts (sometimes the employer lets their employees have merchandise at cost, and you can't make money selling your merchandise to customers at cost). When the discount is misused and given to others outside of the company, the company then has to adjust for this loss and again raise their prices. So, I say, fire the employee that cost the company money: If it was my business, you can bet that I would.

In another store, I have seen coupons used with the same inappropriateness as the associate discount card. I found multiple employees passing around a single coupon to each other that would give them a huge discount. The coupon, however, was intended for one customer one single time in an attempt to get customers into the store. In fact, not all customers were mailed out the same amount of discount, but when an employee found the best one, they took it and shared it with the other staff members. In one such instance I had a strong case against a group of employees: eleven employees, one customer 30% off coupon, and over $3000 in loss. After a very heated debate with the district human resources lady, who believed that I hated everyone, my case was dismissed as a "training issue," although all of the employees said they knew what they were doing was wrong. A few months later I fired most of them due to other losses that they were responsible for, such as stealing merchandise, stealing money, and not ringing up their friends. Although I may seem bitter at times about people who steal, I have seen it far too often—once an employee feels comfortable stealing from their employer, they do not stop until you walk them to the door and promote them to customer.

So there it is: loss prevention in a nutshell. There are so many ways that businesses lose money every year from shrink, but it is the job of one person (or team) to stop the bleeding. Since doing this, I have yet to see the crime rate drop, especially for theft, so there is always room for a good loss prevention person somewhere among the mix. I will warn you, though: every day thieves get smarter and come up with new tools. This means it is your job to constantly be learning and bettering yourself. Now that I have given you multiple ways that businesses lose money, let's talk about how to stop it.

The Good, the Bad, and the Dirty

If you are just coming into the loss prevention world, then you are probably a little overwhelmed by the new world and insight that has been bestowed on you, and are starting to feel like everyone is stealing from you. I am not sure how well I trusted people before coming into the job, but I am sure that I already had a large guard due to being in the Army for a time. The more time that you spend in loss prevention, the less surprised you are that people steal, from an old lady to someone in a wheel chair, a priest, a mother with her children, a store manager—it doesn't matter who they are if they give in to temptation. I have had countless conversations with people wherein I have told them who to watch because they were about to steal something, and they would answer, "They don't seem like they steal." So here is the first and most important lesson: **Everyone suffers from temptation and therefore has motivation to steal**. If you have the idea in your head that only kids who wear backwards hats and pants down to their knees steal, you need to correct that right now. The truth is that there are so many different motivations that trigger people to steal that even someone who you are absolutely positive will never steal just might surprise you.

At the different companies that I have worked for, I am usually good friends with the store manager. This is essential if you want a good working foundation on which to move the store forward; in fact, if you do not have a good relationship with the store manager, then your job will be questioned at every turn. Now, while you may be "good friends," you cannot be blinded from doing your job by your friendship. One of my store managers was faced with a large problem. Their bonus was based on multiple metrics including total shrink of the store, like most store managers' bonuses are. Their bonus would take a $45,000 hit if they revealed the true numbers of their inventory, but by just pretending to have an extra $10,000 of merchandise, they would get their full bonus. I am sure that you are probably thinking, boo hoo store manager, you can live without an extra $45,000; but what a huge temptation that would be. The store manager, a "good friend" of mine, decided to buy $10,000 of merchandise, but instead of taking it home they recounted their inventory so that they would pass with flying colors. A few days after the inventory was over, they voided out their previous sale so that it was as if it never happened. The $10,000 was credited back to the store manager's account and no one was the wiser. Well, no one was the wiser until it popped up on my newly created return spreadsheet. The initial shock stung a little as I was only halfway through my loss prevention career, but the evidence was solid. A temptation of $45,000 was enough to break the store manager's focus and lose a 20-year-long career. Since I was the only person to know about this, I immediately began to try and justify the store manager's actions to myself. Maybe it was a mistake, I thought, or maybe he was buying stuff for a charity event that fell through, or maybe... nope, I knew the truth, but I just didn't want to admit it. The store manager had to be talked to, fired, and prosecuted no matter how many excuses I could come up with. At the time, I not only had a store position, but was also in charge of interrogations that happened within my district. My boss asked me if I needed to have an outside person do the interview, but I was determined that I could do it myself. The store manager's bonus did not come until about a month after the inventory was done, so I had to carry on like nothing was the matter—and it tore me up. Once the day finally came to talk to the store manager, my hands were shaking. Out of personal respect, I wanted to tell the store manager to quit his job before we talked, that way I may not have had to prosecute the store manager, but my job came first every time. Once in the room to start my interrogation, the store manager finally understood what was about to happen and looked at me with such sad eyes. This is the same look that I have gotten from hundreds of interrogations by employees caught stealing, but this was the first time that I got it from someone that I considered a friend. The whole time we were talking I could not help but think of his family, the times we went out to eat for lunch, all of the reasons that I should have let someone else take over the interview but didn't. So here comes rule number two: **NEVER let your guard down by getting too close to the people that you are paid to observe**. The job that you signed up for is very black and white: either you do what you are paid for or you lose your job. I chose my own self-preservation that day and sent a friend to jail. Hey, I have yet to tell you that this job is easy, so why are you surprised? My goal is not to tell you the lighter side of how this job works—although I will in a few more chapters—my goal is to help you understand the profession and what you have to do to make it a career.

Now that we have covered the two most vital rules in loss prevention, and understand that everyone is a potential thief, let's discuss how to put the odds in our favor against temptation. Once you grasp that everyone who has the potential to steal also has motivation, you can begin to fight it. Temptation works inside most people's heads as the bad voice of reason, telling people that it is fine and they won't get caught. Now, if your store has not had an employee fired in a very long time due to theft, then this bad voice of reason sounds pretty convincing; after all, most employees know of someone in the company that they suspect is stealing, and if they haven't got caught, why would you? So now we have temptation on one side and only a small moral compass on the other side of any given employee. No matter how big you believe someone's moral compass to be, they are constantly going through an ongoing battle with temptation. Some days, temptation might sound reasonable. I can tell you with certainty that most employees I have caught started stealing while they were mad at the company they worked for. This type of resentment fuels temptation's argument inside of people's heads and makes the employee feel as though they are owed what they steal. If an employee feels as though they were unjustly written up, should have received a bonus but didn't, didn't get the proper recognition they felt they deserved, or any other treatment that makes them upset about their company, it starts to tip the scale in favor of temptation while their moral compass grows smaller. So now we have the loud voice of temptation on one side and a much smaller moral compass on the other, along with some resentment toward the company; mix in the small dash of invincibility that the employee feels because no one ever gets caught for stealing, and now you have a perfect recipe for an otherwise good employee who will probably steal.

Temptation will always be a loaded gun of an emotion that is hard to fight, and you will never truly be able to get rid of the pressure of it for your employees. You can, however, make sure that temptation is as slight as possible by making sure that your processes are in place for merchandise handling. Doing random audits of an employee's department is one such way to show your employees that you are watching and checking to make sure everything is there. Making sure that cages and lock boxes that are supposed to be locked are actually locked also takes away the temptation that some employees may face. While these simple processes may feel like silly requests that you are already doing, I would challenge any store to do an audit to ensure that it is being done every time. At one of my previous stores, the loading dock was supposed to be locked by the night manager every night. The night manager, being a little overworked, started to give his keys to employees to lock up instead, and on some nights the night manager forgot completely. This was only found out after we had discovered that six employees were taking merchandise out through the dock door almost every night. The case ended up involving about $60,000 of theft. The process and procedure had fallen and the temptation for theft among the dock employees rose. This temptation did send the employees to jail; however, the store would never recover the stolen merchandise. So again I stress the importance of making sure the most simple and rudimentary processes that are in place to combat temptation are actually being followed. This would be a perfect time to go around the store and make a list of things that combat temptation, and then follow up constantly to ensure they are in motion—and for goodness sake, make sure the darn loading dock is locked at night! This may seem like a no-brainer, but trust me, you do not want to be *that* store.

With a limited hold on temptation in sight, we need to move on to the resentment that fuels employee temptation. Everyone gets their feelings hurt, and for different reasons—this is not something that you can fix. The way to make sure that a simple hurt feeling does not turn into a $60,000 employee theft is to make sure you are winning with the open door policy. Hell, call it the "I'll drag you though the door myself if you don't tell me what is bothering you" policy if you need to, as long as you drive it home. While I am not trying to tell you to interfere or get involved with employees' personal lives, if their work is starting to suffer then they may need a pep talk. Since we spend about a third of our time at work, chances are the thing that is bothering them may be something that has happened at work. If you address these work-related problems before they grow too big, you may just save a good employee from becoming a bad one, or a bad employee from becoming an employee that steals from you. In so many interviews that I have done with employees that have been caught for stealing, they recognize that their work suffered after they were upset long before they started to steal. This means that the employees were almost crying out for help, but didn't get it; maybe even the fact that they stole was some sort of cry for attention in some cases. Either way, an employee that seems depressed around your store is not making you any money, so fix the issue to help with your customer service and to stop a potential theft from happening. The last thing that will help with your employees' moral compasses is to show the consequences and reparations of stealing. When an employees' temptation is winning the battle over their morals, the thought of being caught will change the tides. This is not an excuse to celebrate when a dishonest employee is caught for stealing—although I know that some of us do—but to not hide the fact that someone was caught. In two separate stores that experienced employee theft while I was employed, one fired the employee and let them leave out the back door so that they did not see anyone, and the other had the police take them out in handcuffs through the front door. The employees at the first store never even knew that one of their colleges got caught for stealing, and in my opinion that was a huge missed opportunity to show their employees that they will be caught if they choose to steal. By having the employee leave through the front door in handcuffs, you are showing the consequences of stealing and giving your employees ammunition against their own temptations—think of it as helping your other employees chose the right path. I can guarantee that seeing a coworker walk out in handcuffs will have a much larger impact than walking them out of the back door unseen.

Combatting external theft, or shoplifters, is almost an art form to many companies. You can put some of your high theft items on theft preventative tools so that they cannot be stolen, but then the items are not easily attainable by your true customers that want to give you their money. There has to be a happy medium between locking everything up like valuables in a bank, and letting your shoplifters have their way with your store. Although I am a diehard loss prevention guy, I have to say that I cannot stand when I go to a store and find an empty box of something that I wanted to buy, just to then have to hunt down an employee who can get the merchandise for me from the back. Empty boxes are not the way to go for any store, unless the merchandise is something that your store doesn't sell very often: in that case, don't carry it. If your store is losing ten computers a month and you only sell one computer a month, figure out a better way to protect it or stop carrying that item. You are not here to lose money. Each store is different and may need different theft deterrents depending on what is stolen throughout the store. The first thing you should know, obviously, are the main items in your store that are being stolen. Now, if you are a store manager or a loss prevention person, then you are laughing because of course you know what your top stolen items are—but here is where I am going to blindside you and make you that much better. What department manager, area manager, assistant manager, team leader, or any other employee knows what the top stolen items are in their department? They do not have the opportunity to print out a little list that tells them like upper management does, nor do they have a way to sort it by the department that they work in, so it is your job to inform them of this. No, I have not yet found a company that has the store manager or loss prevention person go to each employee and tell them of the top stolen items that they are responsible for, and because of this, another missed opportunity surfaces. I remember going into one store that I was doing an audit at and telling an employee of their top stolen items in their department. One of the items was a little Lego gift bag the size of your palm, easy to conceal if you are a shoplifter. As I told the employee of this item, she interrupted me and said, "That's because it's in a horrible spot on the back wall where no one can see the customers. Can we move it?" I was almost giddy at her response and recommendation, because she wanted to take an active role in helping her department. We moved the item, and overnight it stopped being one of the top stolen items. So here comes the next important rule: **Get everyone in the store actively involved in the loss prevention at your store**. I do not care how good a loss prevention person you think you are, you still only have two eyes at most when there are hundreds of store employees that would love to help—use them. Do not try and deputize your employees to tackle or stop shoplifters, but teach them what to look for to help you.

Imagine for a moment that your store has one to five loss prevention people hired on at any given moment, and then presto—your store has a hundred active participants that are looking out for theft because now the whole store is involved. This is great in theory, but how do I involve a store full of employees that are probably more scared of our loss prevention person than the shoplifters are? Besides, what would it do for our customer service if we started hunting shoplifters instead of doing our jobs? Well I am glad you asked (or, umm, I asked, but only because I know you were thinking it). The following is my secret for success in gaining loss prevention ownership from all employees throughout the store. If your store follows this guideline, then I can promise that you will see a drastic change in the environment of your store.

- **Loss Prevention Open House**
  I have only walked into to one company that has had a system set up to create a loss prevention open house quarterly. This helped open up communication between the loss prevention department and the employees throughout the store. Once employees feel as though they can speak freely to their loss prevention team, it will open the floodgates to tips of possible shrink. Also, employees will feel less comfortable stealing when loss prevention opens their doors and shows them some of the cameras that they have installed throughout the store. While I would hesitate from showing all of your cameras, showing one over a register might deter an employee from stealing cash because they know that there really is a camera watching them. Open the conversation up to the employees to ask questions about loss prevention; this will not only help with their involvement, but also let you know who wants to come to the department to work. Make sure that the employees leave with a good understanding of what suspicious behavior looks like and what the commonly stolen items are, and I guarantee that you will have a plethora of tips about shoplifters shortly after your meeting.
- **Tip Calling**
  Now that you have had an open house and trained employees in what suspicious behavior might look like

(empty bags, looking up at cameras, selecting multiples of the same item, etc.) you can use their newfound knowledge to let you know of any shopper that may exhibit some of these behaviors while shopping. Employees will love the chance to get into the excitement by calling their loss prevention person and letting them know about a guy with an empty duffle bag selecting multiple movies. This type of behavior may seem like "of course they should call me on this," but if you have never trained them to do so then they probably won't. In some stores where I have demonstrated this tip, employees would quickly ask if it was really OK to let us know about suspicious customers and behaviors. These employees wanted to help, but felt like they were stepping on our toes by letting us know. I can't say this enough times: Use the hundreds of eyes throughout your store. In some stores I have seen better results from employees' eyes than from cameras. I remember in one store I had one employee that kept me busy throughout my entire shift almost daily; go figure, she was a fitting room lady and she was darn good! Make sure that employees know that you will not always be able to get to the phone, and even if you do answer it you may be otherwise detained. In these instances, arm your employees with the best ammunition they have: GREAT CUSTOMER SERVICE. Most shoplifters do not want to be remembered; they want to make it in quickly and out quickly with their goods. By having an associate constantly walk up to a potential shoplifter and offer assistance, you are greatly deterring the shoplifter from continuing his actions and fostering great customer service if they are not actually a shoplifter. In one store where we rolled this out, their customer feedback surveys increased almost 10% that month—what store manager wouldn't want that? You phone will be ringing nonstop after your first open house and not all of the tips will be sound—it is your job to train these employees that you are looking more for suspicious behaviors than suspicious people. The more you train them, the more solid leads you will get when you answer your phone. It is also a good idea to track the tips that come in to you and from whom the tips come. That way if you make a large bust because of one tip, you can later congratulate the employee and let them know that their tip was helpful in saving your store's merchandise. Remember that lack of recognition is an easy way to make a good employee a bad one, or a bad one into a thief. Plus, giving them even just a high-five for a job well done will continue to motivate them to help.

— **Anonymous Mailbox**

We talked briefly before about the fact that all employees believe they know someone who is stealing or doing something wrong, but they never know who to tell. Although having the open house will achieve better communication for your employees, placing an anonymous mailbox somewhere in the store will let employees give tips that they may not want to say face-to-face. Think about how it felt to go to a teacher and tell on someone: No one wants to do that, especially if someone else sees. Letting people know that there is a box that they can go to a leave a tip for the loss prevention team completely anonymously will give those who may be timid a chance to speak out. In one store I was helping a friend get acquainted with his new position. We instantly held an open house wherein we spoke of the new anonymous tip box for employees. Later that week when we checked the box, there were three different tips on employees that were stealing from the store. We were instantly able to stop the bleeding from some of the theft going on that we might not have found for months otherwise. This type of box lets your employees know that you appreciate what they think and will follow up; it's huge to them.

— **Known Theft Map**

A lot of the ideas that I have implemented throughout different stores are just a result of my collaboration with other places that experienced something similar; however, the known theft map I created in one store was instantly used throughout the company. Since then, I have been trying to implement this very easy procedure to help others with their loss prevention. I created a large poster-sized map of the entire store and hung it up on a bulletin board. On this map, I outlined all of the different departments so that it was easy to identify the part of the store where each was located. I then placed a box of push pins near the map and a large empty container underneath. Once in place, I asked all of the employees to take any boxes or tags that seemed to be from stolen merchandise and place it in the container while putting a pin in the map where it came from. If an employee found an empty video game box in the men's clothing department, they would simply put the box in the container and put a pin in the men's department near the rack where they found it. If you thought you knew where your shoplifting hot spots were, I can promise that you will be very surprised to find out where some others might be. In one store, after placing the map, we found that items were being stolen and packages left in the pet food aisle on an almost daily basis. Such a weird spot, and yet it was working for the group of shoplifters. Knowing where their base of operations was, we moved a camera to that spot and caught a group that was stealing about $400 in video games and movies a week. Pins stopped being placed in that department after the shoplifters were caught. Woo-hoo, huge win; cost was about $10. I have made many of these maps, some very complex with different colored pins representing different types of items like electronics, hardware, clothing, etc. I have found that some stores require a very basic system so that the employees stay with the program; however, if your employees are very engaged, you can go one step forward and have them write their initials and location found on a tag taped to the empty merchandise. This will help your team quickly identify that a certain type of merchandise is always being found in one particular spot in the store. I guarantee that if you see a customer with that product in the area that you keep finding the package, you will be watching to see what they do. There have also been several occasions where the empty boxes were being found in a stockroom or someplace else that customers could not get into. Guess what, we found a quick employee theft taking place that we would not have found without this map. Before the map was up, the employees that found the packages just thought that it was strange and threw them away, never alerting anyone. As I said before, your one set of eyes just turned into a hundred without having to deputize anyone.

— **Employee Recognition Board**

It is very clear that we all love recognition for our acts when our results are above what is expected. If your employees are going above and beyond what is normally asked of them to create a better store and you are not recognizing them, then shame on you. I would suggest that you create a bulletin board in the back of your store that lists the top three employees that have deterred theft for you from the month before. An example of this would be the three employees that tipped you off to the most potential shoplifters that were caught. Then, on the board, write a few sentences about how each one of those three employees helped saved the store's inventory. In my experience, employees love being up on this board and will even get competitive against their coworkers to beat them out for a spot on the board. This is again one of those things that you can make as intricate or as basic as you want, depending on your store's participation and involvement; I would caution you, though, only start what you will constantly keep up, otherwise your employees will feel that you stopped caring. In one store I worked at, the employees loved the idea so much that I hung a large picture of a mountain on the board and every employee that participated had their own mountain climber. When they tipped my team off to a shoplifter that we caught, their climber would go up the dollar amount that they saved the store; or if they were able to deter a potential shoplifter because of great customer service (e.g., the shoplifter ended up dropping the merchandise out of their own purse before leaving the store), the employee would get to climb that dollar amount up the mountain. Within the first month, the employees' tips ended up saving the store almost $20,000. With the help of a very on-board store manager, we were able to make milestones that employees could reach on the mountain to receive a gift card to the store. Well darn Alan, this sounds like it is going to cost me a ton of money. Yeah, it might, but I can tell you that I ended up handing out $80 in gift cards that first month and at the same time saved the store $20,000 in merchandise. You can decide where to put your milestones, but the point is that employees could be recognized for taking care of their store. I also had an individual story for each of the three employees that saved the top amount of money for the store. Employees were constantly checking their progress and trying to become one of the top people. This board went above the hope to get LP awareness throughout the store—it motivated employees to constantly have their eyes open to their surroundings. Since this store, I have traveled to a few others and have started this same practice, and the results have been amazing. I am happy to say that in one company, this tool was passed out as a must-do throughout an entire region almost overnight because of the results seen in every store that used it. It gave some of the employees the push they needed to inform loss prevention of a potential loss to the company. Employees would also go up the mountain if they saved the store money by letting us know of a potential employee theft as well, further driving home an LP environment throughout the store. If your store needs help with this, then reach out to me; I'm always available to talk about great ideas, especially if they are mine.

— **Over/Short Tracker**

One company that I worked at seemed to have a lot of great tools available for loss prevention personnel; this was not the case everywhere, though. In this one company, they had an automated system for tracking cash theft from employees at the register. It was very simple to use and only took a few minutes each day. The results showed one potential employee theft every few months. It would note which cashiers were on which registers on the days that the registers were short. After one employee had been flagged multiple times, it would have you look at some of their transactions to see what was going on. A lot of companies believe that this only helps the profit of a store and not necessarily the shrink of a store, so they do not spend much time on this type of offense. I say, hogwash; if an employee is going to steal $20 bucks at their register, then they are probably also stealing merchandise from you. Besides, they are still stealing $20 from you. When I went to my first company that did not have this tool in place, I made one using an Excel spreadsheet and a few dozen codes. The cash office would send me a list of registers that were short the previous day and I would throw the numbers into the spreadsheet. After the first month, I found three associates that had been on registers that were short every single day. While my boss at the time was very skeptical of the results that could emerge, later that month I was able to fire two of those employees for cash theft and one for merchandise theft. Vindication was mine, and my makeshift program was a success. The next month, a district of stores tried out my program for a straight month to see if they would have similar results. A third of the stores were able to catch employees stealing using the program, and most of the stores that caught someone had not caught any dishonest employees for years prior. Besides making my program look like a success, it showed that we as a team of loss prevention agents were not looking the right way to catch certain thieves. For a loss prevention group in a company to be successful, we must all collaborate and share what things work for us so that others may try them. Could you imagine if every company was able to collaborate on their theft deterrent ideas? While thieves get smarter daily and find new ways to steal, we would have the upper hand by sharing our ideas that had been proven to work.

— **LP Meetings**

Every store in every city across the United States has their own makeup of shoplifter that likes to steal from their store. Without being biased, racist, sexist, ageist, or any other "ist," each store has a certain type of shoplifter that primarily likes to shoplift from that particular store. This does not mean that these are the only people that shoplift from there, just that the primary makeup of shoplifters are such a type. Just as a toy store normally has children that shoplift and a beauty store typically has females that shoplift, you must know and understand your primary shoplifter to be effective in your store. Some years back, I moved to a new state where I only knew one person. I quickly began in the loss prevention profession again and went to work. The problem was that I had no idea of the city that I lived in or the type of people that would steal from this new store environment that I was in. Everything was different for me, such as the layout of the store, the type of merchandise, surroundings, you name it. I had no idea except for one thing: I was good at loss prevention and I wanted to be the best at this new company. I went out and befriended all of the other loss prevention people in different stores around me throughout the city, some of which were in direct competition with my store for sales. Every one of the loss prevention people that I talked to seemed to be full of knowledge and had a willingness to help. I decided to gather all of us up and host a meeting once a month. The first meeting that I held brought in loss prevention people from all over the city, as well as police officers, a district attorney, and even some store managers that were curious as to how they could help with their stores' losses. We all brought in pictures of known thieves, stories of new theft devices, and other information that was helpful to us as a whole. I was able to figure out that day that one group that was stealing from me weekly was also stealing from a store down the street on the same days. The police never made it to my store in time to get the crooks, but if I had known that the thieves would be just down the street a few minutes later I could have sent the police there. I didn't know it yet, but I had just started one of the first Organized Retail Crime units in the state. ORC (organized retail crime) groups are usually a team of shoplifters that take a large amount of merchandise from you quickly so as not to be caught. They are usually too large in number to stop them all, and if you do try and stop one, they will more than likely all jump on top of you. My group of loss prevention people quickly got a mind of its own and was soon headed up by the local police. Once a month this team would (and still does) meet to discuss unknown thieves to try and figure out who they were. They would also share different theft devices that they had found on shoplifters so that everyone could learn from the experience. I remember I saw my first purse with aluminum foil wrapped inside at one of these meetings; I had no idea until then that the foil would stop the door alarm from going off if there was a security sensor inside. Now this type of information seems common, but this was years ago; think about what new tools are out there now and ask yourself if you truly know about them all. If you don't, start an LP meeting or find one in your city. I have since started multiple meetings in different cities and only good knowledge has come from them. In one city, I was told that the local college had hazing days wherein they made their participants steal from certain local stores. This information was priceless; when the time came for the "hazing days," I had a team ready to stop the group.

So there you have it: some of my favorite fixes to help stores from losing so much of their own merchandise. There are, of course, many more ways, but any store that can successfully implement these procedures will see a great deal of change in their inventory numbers. Remember that while shoplifters will continue to evolve, so must your knowledge. The best way to combat this is by having a big, well-informed team that is constantly sharing ideas and knowledge amongst themselves.

Suspicious Behavior

For those of you that are currently in the life of loss prevention, most all of the following will already be second nature to you; however, if you are new to the scene, some of these may open your eyes as to what to watch for.

Suspicious behavior is what alerts us to start watching someone for stealing. You should never watch a suspect because of their demeanor, because you will miss out on catching the real threat. Too often have I heard, "Hey Alan, you should watch them, they are going to steal. They are dressed like a crook." What?! That doesn't even make sense, unless you can honestly humor the idea that crooks all go to the ThievesRUs store to pick out their wardrobe. No, clothing very rarely helps you to identify a crook; there are, of course, exceptions to the rule. It does not matter what a shopper is wearing, nor what a shopper is looking at to buy, and please never say, "They can't afford that, they must be about to steal." These are the silly preexisting stereotypes that you have inside of your head as to what a shoplifter looks like, and guess what, you are wrong. The truth is a shoplifter can come from any way of life, have any type of clothing style, be of any age, gender, race, etc. The only way to help narrow a store full of shoplifters to find the few that are about to engage in criminal acts is to watch their behavior. While in the military, and ever since, I mainly studied human nature and the interactions between people. It is not uncommon to find me on a bench in the mall watching people as they pass by. No, I am not looking for anyone stealing, nor am I some creeper; I just like to watch as interactions unfold between friends, acquaintances, and perfect strangers. You can learn a lot about how people truly are just by watching from the background as they live out their lives. You will quickly pick up on different signs that they will show when they are feeling certain emotions. The same is true when trying to spot a shoplifter.

One of my favorite things that I like to teach new people who come into loss prevention is that most Americans touch their face when they are lying. This works because when you start to feel guilt, there is this natural reflex to touch your face in some way. I know it seems crazy, but try it out. Ask a friend something you know they will lie to you about and watch as they scratch their chin, brush off their forehead, wipe their nose, grab their ear or anything else that would constitute as touching their face; but for goodness sakes, don't tell them that you know they are lying. Again, this type of response only works for most Americans; there are a multitude of tells that a person can have instead. One of my buddies, who has been like a brother to me for years, always touches his elbow when he is lying. "Hey Alan, you should have seen me last night man. Tons of girls were asking me for my number" (touching his elbow quickly, then dropping his arm). "Yeah I started to tell them I was married so they would leave me alone but then one started paying for all of my drinks." (Touching his elbow again and then dropping his arm.) The story usually goes on for a few minutes with about four or five different elbow touches; I love the guy and always invite him over for Texas Hold 'Em nights. So how do you make this new knowledge work to your advantage? Well my buddy would never steal, at least I don't think he would—but if he did, once he was in front of the merchandise that he intended to steal, he would more than likely touch his elbow. Weird, right? I know, but this would be his feeling of guilt outwardly showing. The same goes for your typical shoplifter who touches their face once they have found what they came in to steal. It will not be a long touch, because again, it is involuntary, but it will most likely be there. And here you thought my time spent watching people at the mall was a waste, ha. This sign of guilt by no means says that your suspect is in fact a shoplifter; it's just one of many behaviors that you should watch out for.

If you are not impressed with the ninja training that I am trying to do for you, then I will give you the more traditional behaviors that shoplifters engage in:

— **Looking up at cameras**: So many times you have been inside of a store shopping with the thought of cameras watching you completely eluding you. This is because we are not worried about what others may see us do; after all, we are just shopping. Shoplifters, on the other hand, want to make sure that their actions are not caught on camera, so they will constantly look up to see if they can be seen by any of the cameras. If the shoplifter does see a camera, they will more than likely go to another spot in the store and look up again until they find a perfect spot. This will unfortunately make other loss prevention people look guilty as well, because we are always looking to see what other stores have that we don't. Trust me, I have been watched many times when I've gone to a store. This type of behavior is one of the most important things to watch for in a suspected shoplifter. If you see someone dodging cameras, then there is a good chance you want to see what they are going to do as soon as they feel like they are out of sight.

— **Selecting multiples of the same items**: What was the best movie out last year, did it have some sort of Marvel superhero in it? Chances are that this will become a main theft item throughout stores. One important thing to remember is that no matter how good the movie is, there should be no shopper that needs four copies of it. While I have seen some people buy several copies of a particular movie to give as presents, this is far from the norm. If you see someone pick up four copies of a very popular movie, this should tell you that they probably have an alternative plan to buying them. Shoplifters like to select multiple copies of items, like movies and games, because they feel as though they will not be caught once they put one of the copies back.

"You stole a movie Mr. Shoplifter."

"No, I put it back right there."

"Yes, but the other four copies are in your pants." Trust me; this has happened more times than I can count. You can bet that this type of shoplifter already has a certain place that he pawns his stolen items and makes about 25% of the value if it is still in original wrapping.

— **Staying away from employees**: Have you ever gone inside of a store and had to hunt an employee down because you just needed a little help? Although we typically all tell the employees that "I'm fine, thanks" when they ask us if we need any help, we like knowing that they are there in case we do have a problem. I go to a hardware store down from my house about once a week and they always ask if I need any help when I walk in. I tell them "no" because I want to feel competent that I can find what I am looking for, but then a few minutes later I always have to hunt one down to show me where the stupid hidden item is. Shoplifters are always on the lookout for employees and will stay far away from employees throughout their visit in a store (normally this is the case; however, sometimes shoplifters do try to overly befriend employees, too). This type of shoplifter will see an employee coming and instantly change paths so that the employee does not get too close to the shoplifter. The best way to combat this type of shoplifter is to have the employee continue to give great customer service. I usually have the employee say something like, "I love that orange shirt you are wearing, and it really goes well with your eye color. I have another shirt over here that might look really good too that would go with the jeans you are carrying." This statement does two things: first, it lets the customer/shoplifter know that you will remember them, from what they were wearing to their eye color, and second, it lets them know that you know what they have that they might want to steal (the jeans). If the shopper is not a shoplifter, well then you probably just increased your sales for that transaction, so still a plus. I have very rarely seen a shoplifter steal after having an employee say something like that to them—normally they will drop the items and leave the store quickly.

— **Empty bags or purses**: Who in the world needs to go shopping with a beach bag as a purse with nothing inside of it? I know that some of you will say that it is common to have an oversized purse when you go shopping, but if it is empty then you don't need it. About half of the shoplifters that I have caught that used a purse to conceal their stolen merchandise already knew what they were going to do before coming into the store, and emptied their contents out before coming in. This not only let them steal more, but also hid any evidence of who they were in case they needed to throw their purse and run. With a good PTZ system (pan-tilt-zoom cameras), I have even been lucky enough to see shoplifters empty their purse before walking into the store, or hand off all of their purse's contents to their friend so that they would have an empty purse to start with. This is almost an automatic shoplifter; just get ready to be hit with the purse once you try and stop her. Sometimes the shoplifter doesn't even bring in a purse, but grabs one off of the shelf instead and empties the packaging, then uses it to conceal their stolen merchandise. They will almost always say that they came in with the purse, too. Since guys do not usually carry purses (although I have seen some who do), they typically use backpacks or store bags. It was always very exciting for me to see a guy walk into a store, go to a register that was not being used, and grab a handful of the bags that you would get when buying your items. They would then use these bags to fill up to their hearts content before leaving the store with the unpaid-for merchandise. Try to lock up your store bags when they are not being used, or at least try to make them a little less accessible; this will greatly decrease your chances of being stolen from this way. And if you see someone with a handful of store bags hanging out of their pocket, for goodness' sake watch them. Also, tell your cashiers to let you know if a person walks into the store and goes directly to them asking for a bag. Most cashiers will not think twice about this request and will hand over a bag to the shopper, and later the bag will be used to conceal merchandise.

— **Not looking at price or size**: Hmm what size pants am I again? Oh yes I'm a... wait I'm not going to discuss that, but I guarantee that I will look several times at the size of pants when I am shopping for them. A shoplifter that is stealing clothes typically is going to sell the clothes later on (or attempt a fraudulent refund), so they do not care exactly what size of clothes they are grabbing; as long as the price on top says expensive, they are happy. As a shoplifter cruises through the clothing department, you may notice that they grab an item here and then another over here, never looking to see if they have the right size and sometimes not even looking at the price. In fact, it may seem as though they are grabbing clothes the moment that their eyes see them without giving them any thought. There are only two types of people that shop this way: the first is of course a shoplifter because they are just in it for the money, and the second is a teenager who is letting their parents buy them their clothes (the teenager will typically look at the size, just not the price tag). I have been fooled many times into thinking that I had a shoplifter only to find them hand off all of their clothing to their parents once they were done selecting the merchandise. This type of behavior is very common among shoplifters, so if you see it happening, a little alarm should go off in your head.

— **Wearing inappropriate clothing for the weather**: If it is cold out we typically wear jackets, and if the temperature is in the 90s we normally do not wear our ski outfit in public. A lot of times, shoplifters will go against this nature because they have other plans. If is snowing outside and you see someone come in not wearing a jacket of any kind, there is a chance that it is a shoplifter about to steal a jacket. They will put it on and leave the store like they had it all along. If they are wearing a large jacket on a hot summer day, they are possibly going to use this to conceal their merchandise. Be careful with these types of behaviors, because I can almost guarantee that the merchandise will be sweaty if it comes out of a jacket that a shoplifter is wearing when it is burning hot outside. By the way, invest in hand sanitizer for your office and always use it; I have met a lot of shoplifters that had some really funky things wrong with them.

— **Keeping a bag in a cart unzipped**: Getting out of a car and coming into a store wearing a backpack should already send up a warning sign: "Why wouldn't the shopper just leave their bag in their car" should play in your head. Once inside the store, if the suspect places the bag in the bottom of a cart, another warning flare should go off for you. These types of behaviors do not mean anything yet; however, once the suspect unzips the bag and continues to walk around the store and select merchandise, you most likely have a shoplifter. Just because you want to bring your bag in to a store doesn't mean too much, but once you unzip the bag you can easily conceal the selected merchandise inside of it. Chances are that this type of shoplifter will be very calm and has done the same thing many times before. I will caution you though, stopping people with bags and backpacks can get very dicey because only they know what is inside the bag; I will speak more on this later on.

— **Grabbing small concealable items, then going to the fitting room**: Those darn fitting room thieves. Every company has their own policy on fitting room stops—and this is for good reason, because I have seen a lot of good loss prevention people make bad stops because of it. Your fitting room thief knows that you cannot see them inside of the fitting room, so they use it to conceal their selected merchandise. No, there are no cameras allowed near the rooms, nor can you see inside of them, so it makes it very hard to know exactly what a shoplifter is doing or where they are concealing their merchandise. These types of shoplifters will normally pick out what they want to steal, and then grab a piece of clothing so that they have a reason to go in the fitting room. Once the shoplifter comes back out, their desired merchandise is gone (concealed) and the crime is done without witnesses. The best way to combat this type of behavior is to have a fitting room employee who does not allow non-clothing items into a room. Most customers will be fine with this policy, and those who aren't were probably trying to steal from you; besides, why do you need to bring in a $90 razor while you are trying on a shirt? In some stores that I have been to, clothing is the main thing stolen, so it gets a little trickier. If a suspect has selected eight shirts to try on, the fitting room employee only needs to address their selection in conversation. As the employee is opening the door to the fitting room, she takes the clothing, scans through it, and then says something like, "Wow, I like all eight of these shirts. You are going to have a hard time deciding which one looks best." You can bet that a potential shoplifter is going to instantly get upset that they were thwarted before they had a chance and will probably just leave right then. Remember, a shoplifter does not want anyone to know exactly what they have so that no one can tell if they are stealing. If you are going to try and stop a shoplifter with an apprehension, the best thing to use is a notebook. While the suspect is selecting the clothes that they want to take into the fitting room, make a note of what type of merchandise and how many pieces. If the shoplifter goes in with one blue shirt, one white shirt, three pairs of jeans, and a black pair of shoes, but then leaves a few minutes later without some of the merchandise (and it is not left inside of the fitting room), they probably stole that merchandise. Sometimes we forget exactly what the suspect brought inside of the fitting room, so we need to keep our notes in order to remember exactly what is missing. It will not help if the suspect comes out wearing our blue shirt over their own if we don't remember that they brought one in.

— **Distraction**: A lot of times when a team comes in to a store with the intent to steal, one of the members is there to distract the employees. This member of the shoplifting group may not touch any of the merchandise, but is still prosecutable in almost every state. They might serve as the "lookout" to make sure that an employee is not coming while their counterpart is concealing the merchandise. They might be the "cover" and will shield any camera from seeing what is happening by holding up a large item or holding their jacket over the other team members. They may also work as the "talker" to distract an employee from checking on the member who is stealing. In one such store, I caught a "talker" who engaged in a heated conversation with one of my employees at the door who was supposed to be checking receipts. As they were talking, the other members left the store without paying for the merchandise. Both were later caught and both were prosecuted. The distraction member will almost always fight that they never touched the merchandise so they cannot be in any trouble; however, the law in most states is very clear that any knowledge that they have about a crime taking place is reason enough to charge the member. The easiest way to explain this is the getaway driver for a bank heist; they knew what was going on and assisted with the theft. Although they did not touch the money, their active knowledge of the crime and the fact that they also assisted is reason enough to charge them as well. Boom jerk, you are a thief and you were caught, so deal with it.

— **Constantly readjusting their purse or pockets**: There is no reason that you have to move your makeup from one pocket of your purse to another, and then back again, especially if you are doing this several times throughout your visit inside of a store. This type of behavior is usually leading up to a shoplifter trying to find the perfect spot in their purse or pockets to conceal merchandise. You will typically see this type of shoplifter set their purse down to rearrange all of the contents, while sometimes putting unpaid merchandise inside as well and pretending that it is their own. They think they are sneaky, but if you were keeping a list as to what they were selecting previously you should know quickly what they stole. This type of shoplifter will almost always tell you that they had no idea that they were stealing—trust me, they all say that, and almost all of them have a record already. Don't fall for the sad stories! About 95% of your shoplifters will tell you that they have never stolen before, but shoplifters normally only get caught about 10% of the time. This means that your "first timer" has probably stolen from you at least nine times prior. If you want a true story, then know that a shoplifter will undoubtedly lie to you.

— **Staging**: Staging is one of the fun times when you know that a climax is just about to happen. This is when one party comes into a store and places several items into another piece of merchandise or container. Then a second member comes into the store and steals that one item, or they may even buy the one item but fail to tell the cashier of the other hidden items inside. In some stores, the container used to conceal the merchandise is a trash can or a large plastic container. After the first member places the items inside of the container, they will normally leave the store and hand off the baton to the second member. If you can get the two suspects meeting outside on camera, it is an easy case for the District Attorney to prosecute. The second member will know exactly what item the merchandise is stored in because the first member told them or showed them a picture of where it would be. The second member will not look inside of the container and will probably purchase the item; if caught, they will pretend to have no knowledge of the items inside. Umm, duh, it was ten times heavier than it should have been—but you need more information before you can prosecute them; that is why having video of the two members talking outside is crucial. If caught, the first member will say that they did not walk out of the store with the merchandise so they are not in trouble; again, learn your local laws, because the act of "concealing" is illegal in all states that I have worked in. This means that as soon as a shoplifter puts merchandise into their pocket, purse, or in this case a container, they have in fact committed a crime; and while you will probably not stop someone for just concealing, it lets you now prosecute both parties in this type of shoplifting.

— **Untied shoelaces**: Have you ever seen a shopper come into your store with his shoelaces untied, and wanted to yell at them to tie their shoelaces before they fell, mostly because you know how much it costs to have a customer accident? Well, if the shopper is going to the shoe department with their current shoelaces untied, it should raise a huge red flag. This is a practice used by many shoplifters that want to steal shoes quickly before they are seen. They go into a shoe department without tying their shoes and in some cases without shoelaces at all; this way it is easier to take them off and put on a new pair quickly. Speaking of shoe thieves, most shoe theft happens on rainy days, so watch for this type of behavior. On rainy days, shoplifters with old shoes will notice that their feet are getting wet because of how old the shoe is and will desire a new pair, thus a pair of your shoes is presented as an option. The strongest way to fight this type of behavior is to remember what color shoe a potential suspect is wearing. If they had on a pair of nasty black shoes and then after a few moments in the shoe department they leave with white sneakers, they stole from you unless you have a register in the shoe department, which only a few stores actually do. And just remember: when it rains, more shoes are always stolen.

— **No sign of a wallet**: This is another one of those crazy Alan tips that you won't see in any textbook, but I promise that it works more often than not. If a potential suspect is already showing signs of suspicious behavior, and you can tell that they do not have a wallet in their back pocket, then they probably do not have the means to pay for anything inside of your store. I acknowledge that not everyone carries a wallet with them; however, it is very rare that a male has his driver's license and money in his pocket. It does happen, though. I am not giving you all a reason to check out people's butts; however, if there is no bulge where the wallet clearly should go in a person's jeans, you might just have one more reason to watch them. Shoplifters like to dump all personal information before they come into your store to steal; this way, if they are caught, they can make up who they are without a way for you to figure out otherwise. I would say that about 90% of the time when a suspect was presenting some type of suspicious behaviors and I did not see a wallet in their back pocket where there was clearly a wear mark from where one had been, they ended up stealing from me. Think of it this way: if you wear a wallet so much that you have a mark on your jeans from where is usually is, but for some reason do not have it today while at a store to buy stuff, where is your money? I can say that I have never been caught "checking someone out," but it is still something you want to use caution while doing. I have seen many police use this method and it does stand up in court as a reason for suspicion in most cases. Luckily my wife knows me well, because every now and then while we are at the store she catches me looking at some guy's back pockets; instead of looking at me like I am crazy, she instantly knows that I believe they are about to steal (and they normally do).

These are the basic suspicious behaviors that shoplifters typically show when they are about to steal. These behaviors by no means say that your suspect is a thief. You still must follow all of the normal steps that you are required to for your company standards before you stop someone; however, if a suspect is showing these types of behaviors, then it gives you a good reason to watch them. These are also the behaviors that you should be writing in your report as to why you started to do continuous observation of a suspect. "The suspect started to look into multiple cameras around the store so I began my investigation of the suspect." One of the most important questions that the defense attorney will ask you, if you are needed to go to court for a case, is "why did you start to watch the suspect in the first place?" I have seen a lot of good cases get thrown out because of silly responses to this question. I have heard things like, "I just knew they would steal," "they look the part," "wouldn't you," and so on; these types of responses will lead the court to believe that you are profiling suspects when they enter the door. Although the suspect may have in fact committed a crime, if the court finds that you were profiling against the suspect, you will be the one found liable and possibly fined. With all of the awards and recommendations that have followed me, the one that holds the most amount of weight is the fact that I have never had a shoplifting case thrown out. If this is a statistic that you have never thought about, then it is time that you did. No matter how big a case is that you get, if all of your hard work is dumped (e.g., catching a suspect, writing the report, burning video, going to court, etc.), then it wasn't worth your time or the company's time to have you do it. This statistic will also play a huge part when one of your cases goes to court: if all of your cases have been air-tight so far, then the defense attorney will be less likely to try and call you in to court and more likely to just try and make a deal with the district attorney instead. You can find out how your cases have done by going to the district attorney's office or just following up constantly on each case.

One of the most important things you can do here is to make sure that the district attorney's office knows who you are and how to get ahold of you. By opening this door of communication, they will quickly call you up if a report seems wrong or a video is not playing for them. If you do not have this open door of communication, then they are likely to just dismiss the case for lack of evidence without giving you a chance to fix it. You have to remember that they are looking at hundreds of cases at a time, so if one of the cases does not seem to be complete then it is easy to throw it away. With this being said, one of the first things that I like to do when I take over a new store or market is to find the attorneys that will be prosecuting my cases and introduce myself to them; I typically find that they still have an old phone number for someone that hasn't worked at the company for five years or so as their main contact. To this day I still have district attorneys call me up and ask about a store that I haven't been to in years because they can't get ahold of anyone else; this is a huge missed opportunity for whomever is now in charge of those stores.

Apprehension Steps

The apprehension steps are the guidelines that your company has asserted to ensure that you have a successful and legitimate stop of a potential shoplifter. These steps are not to be broken while you work for a particular company; however, if you switch to a different company, they may have slightly different rules to follow. Companies tend to have between four and seven steps that you must follow in order to stop a suspect, and if you do not meet these steps then you are to disengage your pursuit and attempt to acquire them before apprehending the suspect. These are crucial, because if you do stop a suspect you have to be prepared to present your case in court; failure to meet these steps could result in your making a bad stop and even getting into legal trouble because you apprehended an honest person. In some situations, you can even be sued because of these actions.

1. **Suspicious Behavior**: This step is not necessarily one of the main steps; however, as stated before, if you do not have a reason to begin your investigation of a suspect, then your motives could be questioned. A lot of companies are beginning to add this step to their list because it is where the investigation actually starts, and it takes away any type of liability that could ensue because of profiling. We all know that we would not watch a young man wearing a hood up because we just felt like he would steal; however, if a person was wearing a hood and a mask inside of your store, no matter what the age, we could consider this a type of suspicious behavior and begin our investigation.

2. **Approach/Entering**: Now that our investigation has begun because of a suspect's behaviors, we watch as they enter a department. This step is not included in a lot of companies' guidelines; however, it can be crucial to making sure you do not make a bad stop. Think about a man shopping for a jacket for a moment. If he enters the jacket department wearing his own jacket but then takes it off to try some on, he may hang

up his own jacket so that he does not have to hold it as he is finding his new jacket. After trying on several jackets, he then goes back to his old jacket and puts it on. Now, if you did not see the man enter the department, you may think, "Bingo, I got you now dirty bird"; but he actually didn't commit a crime at all. This could have easily been a bad stop if you did not see the man enter the department. This type of bad stop happens all of the time with jackets, purses, shoes, even items that a person was returning, among stores that do not have this step included in their procedures. If your company does not have this step added, I would strongly recommend that you follow it anyway—one bad stop could cost you thousands. So the approach is very simple: watch as a suspect enters the department and take note of what they are wearing/have.

3. **Selection**: Selection of the merchandise means that you saw the suspect pick up a certain piece of merchandise from somewhere inside your store. You cannot pretend to meet this step if you just see a suspect with merchandise in their hand—they could have already paid for it, exchanged it, brought it in, and been given it by someone else. Don't risk it. When you are writing your report later on, it is good to include what rack or shelf the merchandise was on before the suspect selected it; this will show the court that the merchandise was clearly presented for sale by your store. I know that sounds silly, but I have had a few defense attorneys argue that the merchandise did not seem to be presented for sale and therefore it was not merchandise that could have been stolen (merchandise inside of a bathroom for whatever reason, outside during a sidewalk sale without signs around it, and inside of the vestibules are all areas of concern here). So when you have selection of the merchandise by the suspect, you want to write in your report, "the suspect then grabbed an Avengers Blu-Ray with his right hand from second shelf down on the movie rack in the Electronics department." This type of selection statement should get you an A+ from the district attorney and leave no question as to whether you saw the selection of the merchandise.

4. **Continuous Observation**: Now that the suspect has the merchandise that you believe they may steal, it's time to win a staring contest. Unfortunately, you have no idea when they might conceal the merchandise or if they will conceal it at all, so you have to be ready. If you have a PTZ system, it is so useful at this time for watching the suspect; however, you must have someone else ready to make the apprehension or else you will lose visibility of the suspect. You can bet that the suspect does not want to be seen concealing the merchandise, so they are going to find a place that is empty of employees and customers. This makes it hard without a good camera system, but far from impossible. Good floor observation is key here, because you cannot always rely on your cameras and some stores do not have any. If the suspect goes around a fixture and comes out on the other side of it without the merchandise, you have no way of telling what happened unless you were able to keep observation of it. Do not try and apprehend the suspect if you did not see the concealment when they went around the fixture—you will only get lucky so many times. The suspect could have dropped the merchandise or staged it for someone else to grab later, and this will end up being a bad stop. If you did see the concealment of the merchandise, then the game is on. You must maintain continuous observation until the suspect leaves the store without paying for the merchandise and to the point of the apprehension. Do not get lazy and just assume they are still going to leave the store with the merchandise. If at any point you lose observation throughout the rest of the steps, you must not stop the suspect; instead, try to regain all of your steps, starting from their entering the department.
5. **Concealment**: Concealment of the merchandise means that you see the suspect put the merchandise that they had previously selected into a place that limits the visibility of such merchandise and makes it hard for employees to see the unpaid-for merchandise. That's my technical answer for the day, but this just means that they put it in their purse, pocket,

jacket, sleeve, pants, trash can, backpack, store bag, under a hat, or any other crazy place that makes it so that you can no longer see the item nor can they pay for it while it's there. In most states, concealment of merchandise is against the law and can be ticketed for by the police; although this is law, I would not try and apprehend a person who has only concealed merchandise unless it is your company's policy. I have been to one such store that did give their team permission to stop once they had concealment because it was easier to stop the suspect inside of the store than outside; however, these cases will rarely get a shoplifting ticket and at most just a concealment ticket, if it is not dismissed in court for lack of evidence that the suspect had intended to exit the store without paying for it. In your report here you should be very clear as to where the suspect concealed the merchandise and what they used to conceal it; this can turn an ordinary aluminum purse into a shoplifting device and change the case from a misdemeanor to a felony in some places. "The shoplifter then took the movie to the shoe department where they placed and concealed the movie in the main pocket of their green purse. The suspect then zipped up their purse and placed the purse back onto their shoulder with the unpaid-for movie still concealed inside." This should be exactly what the district attorney needs to show that the suspect had intent to steal the item from your store. Since there is no register inside of the suspect's purse, and the merchandise cannot be seen by the store, there is now reason to believe that the suspect does not intend to pay for the item. We still must maintain continuous observation of the suspect until the end of the investigation, but now our hearts are pumping a little as the excitement is building. There are a few additional notes about the concealment step, as it is the one to do with showing that the suspect has intent to steal. If the suspect pulls off the tags to clothing that they have selected and then puts the merchandise on, this also is showing intent to steal and should be used as such. Although the concealment never happened if they put the merchandise on, they are still making it hard for employees to tell that the merchandise is theirs, and they cannot pay for the merchandise without the tags still on the merchandise. I have yet to see someone pull tags off of the selected merchandise and then try to pay for it later on. Also, in some bold cases, a suspect may not try to conceal the merchandise and still leave the store without paying for it. In these cases, as long as you maintained continuous observation of the merchandise from their selection to when they attempted to leave, you can still stop the suspect. These types of cases happen when they put merchandise on, or try to walk out with an unpaid-for vacuum (or any type of large merchandise), or push out a large amount of merchandise inside of a cart without paying for it; this happens all of the time.

6. **Passing the last point of sale**: So now we are already contemplating how this stop is going to go. Are they going to fight, are they going to cry, or are they just going to be complacent? Our adrenalin is up, but there is still work to be done and steps to follow. Now that the suspect has selected the merchandise, concealed the merchandise, and we have maintained continuous observation to be assured that the suspect has not put the merchandise down, we must watch as the suspect passes the registers without paying for the merchandise. This step maintains that the suspect is in fact a shoplifter and not getting ready to pay for the merchandise. I have seriously seen women put merchandise into their purse, walk around the store, and then empty it out onto the register to pay for the items before they left. Crazy to think, I know, but when the cashier would politely ask them not to do this in the future, the suspect's response was, "you didn't have any hand baskets in here." Although this type of behavior may be illegal in some states, it made perfect sense inside the suspect's mind. So we must make sure that the suspect walks past the last register toward the door that they are about to exit. If you have a sidewalk sale going on and there is a register out there, you must let the suspect get past that one as well. By the way, I hate sidewalk sales from a loss

prevention standpoint, and you rarely get customer service from a customer standpoint. Keep your merchandise inside where it belongs.

7. **Exiting**: If we have maintained all of our steps to this point, then we are ready to make our stop as soon as the suspect goes past the line that your company has set for you. In some companies, the line is ten feet from the door inside of the store. This gives the loss prevention personnel access to stop the suspect before they go outside, making it much safer for everyone involved. If you are allowed to do this, get ready for a shoplifter to swear that they were just looking out the door to see if it was snowing in the middle of July, but they never intended to actually leave the store without paying for the merchandise down their pants; as long as they have passed the last point of sale (the last register they could have used) and you are following your companies guidelines, then your case is still solid. Some companies ask that their loss prevention personnel wait until the shoplifter gets into the vestibule, past the first door but not out the second. This is a great place to stop a shoplifter because it quarantines their escape and limits their resources; also it makes it clear that they did not intend to pay for the merchandise, giving you a slam-dunk of a case. The main area of concern here is the shoppers that are coming into your store at the time of the apprehension. If possible, have another member behind you ushering the customers to the other open door, this will save you when customers start walking between you and the suspect. Oh, and by the way, you can now call the suspect a shoplifter—but not until this point; remember that when writing your report. Calling them a shoplifter before this point is not accurate and can hurt your case because you are labeling them before they committed a crime. Obviously you are writing the report after you have caught them stealing; however, you need to be writing the report as if you are in the moment and so you should be using "suspect," or even better, "male/female suspect."

I am not going to go into depth on how to stop the shoplifter, because it is widely different between companies. Some companies believe that you should just use the sweet sound of your own voice, others allow for an open hand with moderate force, and there are still some that issue handcuffs and allow for the hog-tying of thieves. I have done them all, and more often than not you can easily get the shoplifter to stop just by sounding confident. While the stores that allowed for a rodeo to happen made for the best bar stories, they were also the ones that could hurt/kill you. When I first got into the loss prevention business, there were few things that I loved more in this world than to go toe-to-toe with a thief; the adrenalin rush right before you stopped them and then almost hoping they would take a swing at you really pumped me up. In the beginning part of my career I was a single dad and it was very common for me to pick up my son from daycare as I was covered in blood; whether it was mine or someone else's didn't matter. I never backed down from a fight and took my fair share of losses and wins, never realizing exactly what I was fighting for. See, if a guy was stealing food because he was homeless and hadn't eaten in a few days, I saw him the same as I did a couple of punks stealing video game consoles to sell on the street; it didn't matter to me. If you stole I would stop you at all cost. Looking back now, I can see that some of those homeless guys wanted to eat as badly as I wanted to catch them, probably even more. Thinking of that, they probably could have done without a punk like me wanting to get into a fight with them over stealing a candy bar. I am saying this because using a confident voice will get most of your shoplifters back with you; there is normally no reason to engage in a fight with a shoplifter although our adrenaline is telling us to do so. So the little voice inside of your head begging for them to pull out a knife so that you can punch them in the throat is probably not the reasonable side you should be listening to—trust me, I have been there several times.

I know a lot of you are saying that using confidence does not always help to stop a shoplifter, and you are right—so trick them. First, when you walk up to a shoplifter whom you are about to stop, make sure that you are standing between them and the door that they are about to leave through. I have seen many lazy loss prevention people walk up beside the shoplifter, giving the shoplifter an open route to escape. By being in front of them, the shoplifter feels much more trapped and is more willing to stop; besides, they feel that if they walk into you, you will grab them and bring them back with force (they normally don't know what you can or can't do, unless they are pros). Next, make sure they know you are confident about stopping them. Bad example: "Umm, I need you to stop because of the stuff you stole." Saying this will let the shoplifter know that you are not confident about stopping them, nor are you sure that they stole anything; they will probably yell obscenities at you and leave. I find that this is exactly how most people talk to a shoplifter when they first start, or when they are afraid of conflict. Good example: With hands out and palms to the shoplifter like you are defending a basketball player: "Sir/Ma'am, my name is (blank) from loss prevention and I need to talk to you about the unpaid movie you have in your pants. Turn around and come this way, please." With your hands, direct them in which way to go. Doing it this way will not give your shoplifter much time to think about what to do next, they will typically turn around and go whichever way you tell them to go. It will also help a great deal if you have another coworker behind you, because it will make the shoplifter think that he will have to take on both of you if he doesn't stop. In a few companies, all members of management or a team of managers are to go to the door when a shoplifter is about to be stopped. While this does take time out of your manager's day, it results in a much safer apprehension with less potential for people to get hurt. If you have a team like this, make sure that one of the members watches the door from behind you so that innocent customers do not get in between you and the shoplifter. Protecting everyone around you should be the main objective every time; the merchandise is only second in priority. Sometimes at this point a shoplifter will still have the knowledge that you cannot physically touch them because of your company's standards. If this does not work, I recommend tricking them.

I would make sure that you clear any method that I give you with your superior before using, as some companies may not like some of my crazy antics. All of the things that I do are to create the safest and best results for loss prevention personnel; however, if your company has a different standpoint than mine, follow theirs. I am not the one writing your check: they are. If, while you are waiting for your suspect to leave the store, you can have one of your counterparts back up the cameras to see what they drove in with, this will help you even more when stopping the shoplifter. In most cases while I am watching a shoplifter, I have someone else back up the DVRs until they find the shoplifter come into the store, then I have them see what car they pulled in with to give me more information during the apprehension. Then when the shoplifter is still about to leave, disregarding my request to stop, I can say one of these: "Sir/Ma'am, if you leave then I will be forced to call the police, giving them your picture and the picture of your green Saturn with license plate number XYZ 123. How long do you think it will take them to find you?" Most shoplifters that were about to leave decide to stop at this point because they know the vehicle is registered to them or their parents, and do not want to show up at home with the police waiting for them. If you do not have the vehicle information, then you could say this, again, with the permission of your superiors: "Sir/Ma'am, the police are outside and I promise that they can tackle you if you do not comply. I don't want to see this get worse; come back to my office so we can talk about it." I didn't lie—the police are outside, somewhere—and yes, the police can use reasonable force if the suspects do not comply with the police. By using this statement, even if the shoplifter was about to get violent, they often comply with my request and turn around to my office. Does this make for a much safer environment instead of the shoplifter getting violent in the front of my store? Yes it does. Using these techniques will greatly reduce the amount of shoplifters that do not want to stop if you are only allowed to use a confident voice to stop them; but again, use caution and permission before doing something differently than you have been instructed by your company.

Walking a Suspect to the Office

So now that the suspect has complied, or you are using a bit of reasonable force; either way you are heading back to the office to do the wonderful paperwork. It's pretty cut-and-dried now, right?! There should be no reason to worry or use caution any longer. Umm, no. Your shoplifter still has their adrenaline up with yours now, and is still debating how to make their escape or at least dump the merchandise so that you can't stop them at all. Some companies tell you to walk beside the shoplifter with one open palm on their back, using the other open hand to show the way. I dislike this method intensely. If you are by yourself, then you need to walk closely behind the shoplifter and have them walk slowly, giving them voice commands as to where to go. Can this open the door for the shoplifter to run? Absolutely, but it will also keep you a thousand times safer. I have seen firsthand a shoplifter being escorted from the side until the shoplifter slowly pulled out a knife from the other side and plunged it into the loss prevention person. In fact, I can show you a scare if you would like to see it. When you are to the side of a shoplifter, you lose sight of what the shoplifter is doing on the other side. Without this "continuous observation," the shoplifter could be preparing for a fight, or dumping the merchandise that they had previously stolen. From behind the shoplifter, you have a clear shot at both of the shoplifter's pockets and can instruct them to keep their hands out of their pockets until you get into the office. Also, if they attempt to dump the merchandise, you need to know this before you get them into the office; nothing is worse than letting a good stop become a bad one because the shoplifter does not have the merchandise on them any longer. In one company that I was at, while walking two male shoplifters back to my office, one of the shoplifters continued to try and put his hand into his pocket. After telling the shoplifter that I would have to use force on him if he did it again, he complied. Once in the office, the men took out their belongings and placed them on my desk. One of them had brass knuckles and the other who kept putting his hands in his pockets had a metal asp. No matter how much training you have, there stands a good chance that you will get a broken bone when hit by an asp; I recommend avoiding it. If I was not aware of the male shoplifter putting his hands into his pocket, I would have been unpleasantly surprised by his weapon of choice.

While walking shoplifters back to the office, it is tempting to choose the quickest path even if that means walking them through departments and between racks. By doing this, however, you give the shoplifters multiple places to dump their merchandise if they think that you cannot see them while they do it. It is much better to take the main aisles to your office even if it is the long way. Also, if a shoplifter believes that there is a rack in between the two of you, they may be more likely to try and run, thinking that the rack will slow you down. Having two or three people walking a shoplifter to the office is ideal and creates a much safer passage for you. The first person is to walk slightly ahead, showing the shoplifter the way to go and also making the shoplifter feel as though they should not attempt to run forward. The second person would be walking closely behind the shoplifter to correct the shoplifter's path, watch their hands, and make sure the merchandise is still being followed. If you have a third person with you, I would have this person to the side of the shoplifter. Not only does this make the shoplifter feel as though they are boxed in, it also allows for the third party to talk to and calm the shoplifter. Remember that the shoplifter may be emotional, attempt to flee, or debating whether to fight—it is good to have a third party do a little small talk on the way to the office. This will also keep the commotion down for the true shoppers throughout your store. If you have a highly emotional shoplifter who is crying while two very serious looking people walk in front of and behind them, chances are you are going to get some looks. This is not the type of environment that you want your shoppers to experience or feel; they need to feel happy and comfortable as they pay you for their merchandise. If a regular shopper feels the drama of your shoplifter, they are inclined to leave sooner and not spend as much; don't let this happen, if possible. Remember, most customers leave their houses and come to the store to get away from stress; shopping needs to alleviate stress, not bring it on.

If your office is close to an exit, then you need to make sure that one of your members breaks off from the train and guards the door to make sure that the shoplifter does not feel like it is an easy escape route, and to try and slow any customer traffic that may get between you and the shoplifter. The best way is to have the lead person break off and guard the door while facing the shoplifter, then the person from behind or the person from the side continues directing the shoplifter to the office door. This will feel like the last chance a shoplifter has to get away if they see an open route to the exit, so be prepared. If the side person has done a good job at making small talk with the shoplifter, it will distract them from even thinking about trying to run at this point. If we have followed the directions, then we should have had a successful walk, and it's into the office we go.

Into the LP Office

So you have watched your suspect portray suspicious behavior, you followed all of your company's steps that have led you to find the suspect has stolen merchandise, your approach of the suspect went well because you were confident, and the walk to the office went smoothly; woo-hoo, it's paperwork time. Let's back up a little first and make sure that our office is ready for a shoplifter. I'm not your mother, so I am not going to harp on the fact that you should have a clean room; however, you should make sure that your office is ready for company. Ask yourself these questions:

— **Is there a clear path from where the shoplifter will enter to where I want them to sit?** If not, then fix it. A shoplifter should not have to walk around your office dodging multiple things that could trip them or be used to hide something they do not want you to see. Also, the more things you have them walk by, the more things that could be a potential weapon used against you if they decide to run. Some companies have you place a camera pointed at where the shoplifter sits—this reduces risk of any type of liability that may happen if the shoplifter begins to allege that you beat them with a phonebook. Make sure that, if you have this camera set up, you are putting the shoplifter in the center of view so that it helps you, and never tell the shoplifter the camera is there if you can manage; they may try to get out of camera view before doing something silly.

— **Where is the shoplifter sitting; do they have access to hide items such as drugs, weapons, or merchandise?** If you have a shoplifter sitting near a bookcase or a filing cabinet with slits in it or anything else that they could push/hide something in, then they will try. On several occasions I have had shoplifters try and hide their drugs throughout my office from where they were sitting. Under their seat, through a vent on the wall, and on the back of my desk, are all problematic places. A good idea is to sit where you have the shoplifter sit, and pretend that you must hide something small within arm's reach. Have the duct tape ready, because you are going to find multiple spots, and as you do you might even find things that have been hidden by past shoplifters.

— **Are there things out in the open that the shoplifter can use as a weapon?** If you have your scissors out and lying on your desk or the stapler within reach of your shoplifter, you have to imagine that these items can be used against you. While you cannot baby-proof your office, you can limit what items can be used against you by your shoplifter. Items that are sharp should be the first items that you have hidden inside of your desk and out of reach of your shoplifter. Any random bats or other weapons that have been confiscated from past shoplifters should undoubtedly not be reachable by a new person that you detain.

— **Do I have any type of non-work-related pictures or personal information up?** When looking around your office, if you have your schedule or your employees' schedule hanging up on the wall, ask yourself what good this might do for a shoplifter. Make sure that phone numbers are not in plain view of your shoplifter, unless you want random death threats in the middle of the night. Any type of non-related pictures that are up may offend someone somewhere, so they probably do not have any place inside of your office for a shoplifter to see and say their feelings were hurt because of it. Also, if you have pictures up of your family or friends sitting on your desk to remind yourself of them, then you should also be reminded that the majority of people that come into your office probably do not like you (i.e., shoplifters). Do not give them ammunition against you; besides, they may know one of them and it would make it really awkward at the PTA meeting that they both attend.

— **Do I have plenty of copies of all of the reports that I need and know where they are?** I cannot stand to go into a loss prevention personnel's office and find them about to do a shoplifting case when they are out of reports. This means that they will have to leave the room to get new copies made, or at least just waste time trying to find where on their computer they have the files saved. You should always make sure that you have blank reports ready to go for your next shoplifter. If for some reason the police are called out quickly to assist you and you are still fumbling around looking for a restitution letter for your shoplifter, you stop looking like a professional. Make sure that you are ready to go every single time so that you can be as quick as needed and do not slow down any law enforcement that may have to come on-site.

— **Do I have a peephole on my door to see who is waiting outside?** When you have a shoplifter in custody that may have come with a friend or ten, chances are they may be looking for them. Heck, they may have even watched you take them to your office and want to try and get them out. I have gotten into multiple altercations with people trying to help their friend in custody escape. If you hear a knock at the door, you should always look out the peephole to see who it is before you open the door. If you look out and no one is there, do not investigate; just like in a horror movie, the bad guy knows that you are not going to open up if he is in plain view. Even if you do not have a shoplifter in custody, you should always look out of the hole before you open the door. Sometimes previous shoplifters want to come back after the incident and "talk" more. They may want to cry and tell you they are sorry, or they may just want to shoot you because you had them arrested; either way, don't engage in the conversation once you are done and have sent them on their way. I had one shoplifter come back a week after I stopped him and had him arrested. This time he was drunk and wanted to fight the guy that ruined his life: me. I opened the door without looking to see who it was and missed a knife coming at me by inches as I opened the door. This was a mistake that could have easily cost me my life and one that I have never made again.

If your office seems ready after asking yourself these questions, then lower the drawbridge and let your shoplifters flood the door into your office. Just remember to constantly recheck these items, as your office can easily change its risk depending on what has been brought in and out. If your last shoplifter tried to steal a knife and you have yet to take it back to the department that it belongs to, where is it now?

When you bring in a shoplifter, make sure that you have a witness with you and that one of you is of the same sex as the shoplifter. This should be your company's policy, and if it isn't, then change it. This is so very important to the safety of your reputation. There will be times when a shoplifter tries to bribe you with money, merchandise, or even favors for you to let them go; these are the same shoplifters that will tell everyone from the police to their spouses or parents that you were the one that offered them a deal. Do not let this happen to you—always, ALWAYS have a witness. I have had many shoplifters offer me "deals" even with a room full of witnesses, and then when the cops came they said that I offered them a "deal." I have even seen them call their family and pretend that the cops offered them a "deal" while in my office in front of me. This causes a very angry husband/father to come banging on my door thinking that he is saving his girl. This also reinforces the need for a camera in your office.

Unfortunately, some people in loss prevention should not be in loss prevention, and some people should not be used as witnesses. If you began to yell at the shoplifter once they are inside of your office, then you are creating a needlessly hostile environment that will not help you get your job done. Even if you have had a horrible day, losing your temper on a shoplifter is not a scenario that will ever help you; besides, you have no idea what has led the shoplifter to steal. If your witness is a person that wants to get involved by speaking to the shoplifter, then you should excuse them and get another witness instead. If your witness is causing the shoplifter to get angry instead of just witnessing, then they could lead your shoplifter into wanting to run or fight. The best thing you can do is to talk calmly to the shoplifter so that you can get your paperwork done and get them out of the office without incident. Also, make sure that your witness is comfortable with being in the room before you have them come in. If you pick someone to be a witness that is scared of conflict, they may feel really uncomfortable being inside of your office while you are processing your shoplifter. In one store, I used to use the same girl to be my witness and then one day she said she did not want to do it while I had a shoplifter. I demanded that she come instantly without giving her a choice because I needed someone right then. Afterwards I found out that she was going to college with my shoplifter and it made it very uncomfortable for her to be in there. Yeah, that was my jerk move #3247, but at least I learned from it.

There is one company out there that has a survey to hand your shoplifter. When I first saw this survey, I hated the idea and had less than pleasant things to say about it. The survey asked such things like "How often do you steal" and "What types of things" and "Why do you feel comfortable stealing here?" The shoplifters rarely answered the questions truthfully if they answered them at all, but it did help keep them quiet as I was working on my report; if they did fill it out I would make a copy and give it to the PD, strengthening my case. It turned out that the district attorney really liked this survey and would use it against the shoplifter if they told him that they had never shoplifted before. "Why did you fill out this survey saying that you shoplift three times a week, then?" he would ask, and then the case was sealed. The survey could also help you identify what areas of opportunity your store might have from a shoplifting point of view. If a shoplifter answers honestly about why they felt comfortable stealing from you, it may open your eyes to some needed changes. Still not loving the survey, I did change it a little to ask a few more questions like "What do you do with the merchandise after you steal it" and "Who do you know that works for this store?" Knowing what a shoplifter does with the merchandise after they steal it will let you know who is buying your merchandise, such as a pawnshop, second-hand store, or a flea market. This information could be very valuable when trying to find your stolen merchandise. Also, if a shoplifter knows someone in your store, there is a chance that the employee may have helped them steal. A few times I have asked the shoplifter who they knew in the store, and it ended up being an employee that had pointed out to the shoplifter the merchandise that they ended up stealing. I have even had some shoplifters tell me that the employee told them that I wouldn't be there that day. Hmm, looks like I will be having an interview with an employee next. Although a survey can be helpful, I find that most shoplifters are more willing to talk to you about these kinds of things than they are to write them down for fear that they are incriminating themselves further. If you don't have a lot of luck with a survey, try at least asking your shoplifter some of those questions; it may be very enlightening.

Shoplifters do still have basic needs that they must be allowed, even when in custody. Check with your own state and city laws, but usually this means that a person is allowed to call their lawyer, police, or for medical treatment at any time—allow them to. I have had many shoplifters threaten to call their lawyer and I told them that I would be more than happy to dial the number for them. I have yet to see any of them actually call their lawyers, nor do I think their lawyers would be able to do anything for them until the police showed up. Some of them have called the police to say that they were being held against their will, maybe to scare me, but I loved it because it meant the police would be there even faster to cite them. And lastly, the fun one: Incarceritis will often make your seemingly healthy shoplifter feel as though they may die without medical treatment. If they feel they need to call 911 because they are dying, let them. All police and paramedics know the term "incarceritis," and although it is not life-threatening, it will make the paramedics come to the scene. This is what happens when a person pretends to be sick to try and get out of a ticket, but it rarely works because it has been exhaustively used. Besides these three things, you also need to know your company's policy on requests for the restroom, drinks, and food. Obviously you need to get the merchandise back from the shoplifter before they use the bathroom or they will attempt to flush all evidence away while in the bathroom; I have seen many toilets overflowing because a shoplifter thought they could flush a shirt or two down the pipes. I would also be careful, because some shoplifters flush their drugs before the police arrive, and you don't really want to have anything to do with that. As far as drinks and food go, this is a very touchy subject. On one hand, you do not want the shoplifter to starve, although I have never seen one starve while working on a report; but on the other hand, they are in your office because they are in custody, so spa treatment is not necessary.

Ready for a horror story? This one still keeps me up some nights. I stopped a guy once for stealing jeans and he put up a pretty big fight. A simple arm hold and I was able to bring him back to the office, where he finally started to comply. Once inside the office, I handcuffed him to the chair to start the processing. I could tell that he was giving me fake information, like his name, but it didn't matter because the police were already on the way. He asked for a bottle of water, so I sent one of my employees to go get one. I began to work on my report after I handed him the water and he turned around a little, away from me. I got up from my desk and walked closer to him to see what he was doing. He didn't seem to have anything in his hands but his water, so I went back to my computer. A few minutes later he began to cry and tell me that he was sorry for everything that he has ever done. This guy started to admit to me that he had done some terrible things to girls in different states. I found it a little odd that he was sharing his life story with me, but it has happened enough times before that I didn't react to it. Then the guy starts to sway from side to side like he was drunk, and I knew something was wrong. I stop the report and began to talk to him, asking him if he was all right. He then said, "I'm scared. I'm not ready to meet my judgment. Hey man, I didn't hurt you and I could have; think good thoughts of me, would ya?" Right then, the police knocked on my office door. As I was telling them what happened, the man passed out. He came to just for a moment to tell them of the drugs that he drank down with the water that I had given him. Soon, my tiny office was full of paramedics and police. Apparently the guy I stopped had just stabbed a person at another store down the street earlier that day, shot a cop in the next city over a few days ago, and had done some unthinkable acts to girls in three different states. He had multiple warrants out for his arrest in multiple states, but none of that mattered as he was lying on my office floor dying, with everyone trying to bring him back to life; and all along all I could think of was that it was me who gave him the water. The man made it to the hospital before leaving this world, and I can't help but to think that without the water, he may not have been able to try and take his own life. Argh, I guess there is no way to really know, and if you really want to end your life then you will find a way to—I just wish it wasn't on my watch. Anyway, you can understand my hesitation in giving people water now, although I still do. The police told me later on that I do not have to give anyone in custody water or food; however, I would still recommend that you follow company guidelines.

Personal bags are sometimes the scariest things that a shoplifter can have in their possession, and as such, are one of the greatest areas of concern for you. There is much debate between companies as to whether they should let their loss prevention personnel handle shoplifters' bags or let the shoplifter handle it themself. If your company is of the standpoint that a shoplifter should get the merchandise out of their own bags, purses, or backpacks and hand it to you, I would wait and have the police do it for you. The safest way to do this is to have gloves on and examine the bag yourself slowly by dumping out the belongings onto a clean surface like your desk; make sure that it is out of reach of your shoplifter, but where they can see you do it. I also prefer this to be on camera when I do it, so I make sure that I am within my camera's range, that way there is no question later on as to what was inside of the bag. Ask the shoplifter if they have anything in their bag that could hurt, stab, or otherwise piss you off before you go through it. This way, if the shoplifter does have a knife, Taser, or gun, they will not be able to get it out and use it against you. It really pisses me off when a shoplifter comes into my office easily just to pull out a weapon on me while in my office. It's like they are coming into my home and trying to rob me, twice. A lot of your shoplifters will have weapons inside of their bags, so you should be ready for it. I have found many weapons, guns, everything you can imagine, and even a ski mask once. A lady that I stopped once was a cat burglar in the area, and apparently left her theft tools in her purse. When I went through it, there was a gun, ski mask, lock picks, and some other craziness. The police had been searching for her for almost a year; go figure, she was caught stealing a "Welcome Home" doormat. Whichever way you decide to go through a shoplifter's belongings, use caution, because you have no idea what is hidden inside.

While we are on the subject, the first thing you should do when a shoplifter comes into your office is to ask them to place the unpaid-for merchandise on your desk (if it is easily accessible and safely retrievable). Then ask the shoplifter to empty their pockets onto your desk as well. This will limit their ability to use anything that they have unbeknownst to you. I also do not allow shoplifters to use their phone while in my office, except on rare occasions. With their phone in hand, they can be secretly texting their counterparts to continue to steal, revealing the location of your office to someone you don't want to come by, or anything else. If they need to use the phone, they can use your office phone; that way you can write down the numbers that they are calling in case you need this information later on. The less you let them have control over usually means the safer everyone is. As I have mentioned before, though, always use respect when talking to them or asking them to comply with your request; if you start to become loud, so will they.

When everything seems calm and you have retrieved your merchandise, work on your paperwork as quickly as possible before the police arrive. I have been asked many times why the police come to my office quicker than most of my colleagues'. The answer is simple: I do not make the police wait for me to get my paperwork done when they get there. The police will quickly get an idea of how you work after they've come by a few times. If they are constantly waiting for you to finish off your report when they arrive, then they will most likely take another call before coming to yours next time. Also, it is a good idea to ask the police if they would like anything different from you the next time they are called out. I have found that for some officers, it helps to have all of the evidence on a disc as opposed to pictures, because they have no way to scan in the pictures for their case; this could result in the DA not having the pictures by the time it gets to them (ie. Pictures of merchandise, receipts, reports, etc). In another district, I found that the police liked having two hard copies of the pictures. This way, they could file one set and keep anther copy for themselves for when they had to go to court. None of the things that I did were asked of me by the police until I asked them what I could do to help them; this let the police know that I respected their time, and in return they respected mine.

Dishonest Employees

No matter if you love catching an employee being dishonest or you despise it, the fact is that it happens a lot and can kill the profit of your business if it is not handled properly. We are going to go over what types of things to look out for when it comes to employee dishonesty, how to handle it, and even some of the basics of the interview process. I have met both loss prevention people and store managers that love and hate this process, but the truth is your company is probably losing more money from employee theft than from shoplifters. Depending on the year and your company, the statistics usually suggest that about twice as much theft happens from dishonest employees as from shoplifters. It seems absurd to think of, but what if you accidently hired a shoplifter as an employee; wouldn't they have free reign of your store all week long with no one to suspect them? Of course we all want to be able to trust our employees and say, "they wouldn't steal." But if we say this, then we have to go back to the beginning and ask ourselves what a shoplifter/thief looks like. Since money is a large motivator for theft, and most people struggle from time to time, all of the merchandise that your employees are surrounded by that they can't afford is going to tempt them to do something dishonest. This is not to say that every employee is a thief, but it does mean that almost every employee is tempted and therefore has motivation that they may give in to. If you still say that your employees are the honest ones, think about this: most of your shoplifters are employed somewhere. Usually the hardest part of believing that an employee is stealing is that you hired them; after all, you wouldn't hire a thief, right? I can humbly tell you that after the countless interviews I have conducted, after the years spent in this field, although I have spent hours just watching people's actions, I have still hired people that have turned around and stolen from me. It's a hard pill to swallow, knowing that you are your own culprit of shrink because you hired your own thieves; but you cannot control what others are going to do, nor do you know what obstacles they are going to face in the future. So if you do catch an employee being dishonest, do not take it personally or dismiss it—take the opportunity to appreciate that you found it sooner rather than later and fix what you need to. These next tips will help you stop the bleeding of your store's money:

— **Package checks**: Package checks seem to be one of the hardest things for people to do, and yet they can quickly stop a dishonest employee from stealing or deter one from starting. At every company that I have been to, somewhere in their policy and procedures it states that the company is allowed to do random package checks of their employees when they are leaving the store. This rule is in place to keep people honest and make sure that the people planning to do something dishonest know that they may be caught. This only works, however, if random package checks are being made. Most people, including myself, hate asking employees to open up their purse as they are leaving for the day. Although it does feel a bit intrusive, this is a necessity. If an employee knows that they are home free once they put the unpaid merchandise into their bag, this takes away some of the fear that you want them to have when they are thinking of stealing from you; you want them to know that they will be caught if they steal. One of the most important rules about package checks is to not pick and choose who you check—if you are going to do checks that night, then do everyone that passes by. You will quickly get yourself into trouble if you skip over all of the nice older ladies and then stop the teenage guy to package check. Also, mix up when you do it and on which days if you are not going to do it every night; this way your employees will not see a pattern as to when you are going to do your searches. As you are doing them, keep a close eye on the employees that see you doing them and then decide that they are not ready to leave for the night. Most times when a dishonest employee has merchandise they do not want you to see and they see you at the door, they will turn around and drop the merchandise; if you see someone that matches this behavior, follow up to see what they may have put down. If you do find an employee with merchandise and they say they already bought it, ask them for their receipt; do not just take their word for it. If they have their receipt, then great, but if they fail to present it, then you can hold the merchandise for them until tomorrow when you can look up the transaction. Chances are that if they stole the merchandise, they won't come back in the morning. I would caution against trying to stop them right then as a dishonest employee, because you do not have your evidence yet. If you try and stall them so that you can look up the transaction that night, it could be perceived as you apprehending them and this could turn ugly if they did in fact buy the merchandise. However, if you have already met your steps to prove they did steal the merchandise, stop them right then and prosecute them.

— **Going out the wrong door**: Most companies have a certain door that employees are supposed to use when entering and leaving the store. This has many uses, such as making sure that you know when your employees are leaving and entering for their shift. If you have an employee constantly going out a different door than the one that is assigned, follow up with them and make sure that they start to comply. If they still are sneaking out a different door, then find out why. They may be trying to not be seen walking out with unpaid merchandise; maybe they think one door does not have a camera, or they know that you are doing package checks at another door. Investigate as much as you can to see what is making them want to go out the other door. If you still do not see anything and the employee is not following directions, consider terminating them. Employees that are not following company rules, especially ones that are in place to prevent shrink, do not care about the success/failure of the company; they will not help you to achieve your company goals, but will instead hamper them. I know this may sound harsh; however, if an employee is deliberately being disobedient about normal rules set in place to prevent shrink, what else are they not following that is causing shrink? Also, once other employees see that they are allowed to go out other doors, it will cause your employees that want to steal to also go out doors where you are not package-checking; this will completely undermine the rules that you have set in place to prevent shrink.

- **Empty packages**: Empty packages of merchandise that are in a stock room or someplace else that a customer does not have access to need to be followed up with and addressed. If you find an empty package of razors in the stock room that you keep electronics in, you need to ask yourself how it got there. If you have a good camera in place with a DVR system, then backtrack until you can find who brought them in there. Chances are you may not have a perfect camera angle, and in that case ask your employees why they are there. You will most likely be told that no one knows, or some employee found it as trash and so they put it in the stock room; neither one of these stories makes any logical sense, so you will need to start an investigation. If you can, move a camera into that area. A covert camera, a camera that is hidden and out of sight from employees, is the best to use in this situation; if you do not have a covert camera, try and place a camera behind a vent or above a tile with a small hole cut out. For some reason, one of your employees finds it safe to steal in that area and it is most likely because they know there is no camera around. By hiding a camera in the area, you may be able to catch the employee when they steal again.
- **Transaction history**: Transaction history is very important when dealing with dishonest cashiers. Depending upon the information that you can get from the reports your company uses, this may be one of the easiest ways for you to identify a potentially dishonest employee. These reports are only as good as you know how to use them, so make sure that whoever is looking over these reports knows what they are looking for. If the report shows you how many times a cashier does a "No Sale" during their shift and one cashier is much higher than the rest on average, you should investigate to see if they are taking money from the register when no one is looking. Pull up the times they are doing the No Sales on camera to see if anyone is around. If one employee is discounting merchandise much more often than the others,

see if the discounts happen for certain customers; they may be giving themselves or friends a great discount when they come in. If a cashier does more Voids than most on average, look up those transactions to see what they are voiding out and if it should be voided. They could be voiding out a transaction that their friends just made so that they will not be charged for the transaction, or they could be voiding out a cash transaction with no one around so that they can pocket the money. If your reports show refunds, see what employee does the most amount of refunds without a receipt being present; most companies that I have been to indicate a non-receipt refund with an asterisk beside it—if you do not know your reports, well then it's time to learn them. The list of what you can uncover with these reports goes on and on; the problem is that most people do not know how to use them and because of this they do not spend much time on them. If you do know how to use these reports, then I would suggest making a simple Excel spreadsheet to enter the data so that you can plot the top offenders of each from month to month; if you don't, you may not remember that your top offender is showing up just about every single month on something and is probably stealing from you. If you are not the one working on these reports, it's a good idea to make sure that the person who is knows what they are looking for; challenge them and ask them to show you what each report is looking for. Most stores that I have audited that have not caught a dishonest employee have not looked at these reports in a very long time, and the person that was supposed to be looking had no idea what to look for. These reports are there for a reason, and will show you who is not really a part of your team—spend some time on them.

— **Over/Short report**: If your company has a report that is tracking cashiers that are showing up on registers that are losing money, then great: you are ahead of the pack. If your company does not have a report that shows this, make one. Here is the deal: If an employee is stealing money from the register and is not getting caught, they are going to do it again and again and again. They will eventually tell one of their friends, who will also start to steal money from the register because no one is looking. A lot of companies do not put much stake in losing money from the registers because it only affects profit and not shrink; however, having an employee that I once interviewed admit to stealing more than $100,000 within two years makes me think that all companies should put a little more weight on this type of theft. If you are not savvy with Excel, find someone who is and put a simple report in place to show you who is on a register when it's short. After a few short registers, it should start to show you a pattern of who has most likely been stealing money from you. In one company, as soon as I released my little Excel program, almost every store in the district caught a dishonest employee in the first month. That means that they are out there ready to be caught as soon as you put some effort into it. Don't forget that someone probably showed them how to steal money, too, and that somebody is probably still at your store as well. If you do an Excel sheet, make sure to have the report flag when an employee has been on a short register more than a couple of times. Also, have it track from month to month, because a dishonest employee is not going to stop just because it's a new month. I will show a few pictures of one such program that I have made at the end of this book. It only takes about five minutes a day to enter the information, and the wealth of knowledge that you can learn from it is well worth it.

— **Anonymous box**: An anonymous box is simply a box put somewhere that lets employees have a way to tell on their counterparts without being in the spotlight. This system works, especially if the employees do not want to talk to the loss prevention person directly. Make sure that your employees know where you put this box, and make it secure—think of it as a locking mailbox with a small slit in it. You will soon get random tips from employees who believe someone is stealing or doing something wrong. Not every lead will bring you a dishonest employee, but I guarantee that some of your employees know of another employee who is stealing. A lot of my leads that were generated this way said that the employees would brag about it after work to their friends—some of those friends were not amused, and gave me the tip. The box let these employees give me the tip without being directly involved in the situation. When you put up the box, put a letter next to it explaining what types of things you want your employees to tell you about. I will put a sample letter at the end of this book.

— **Suspicious behavior**: Employees who steal will probably present the same type of suspicious behaviors as a normal shoplifter. If you find one of your employees grabbing random merchandise and then leaving the department it belongs in just to hide it in a place without a camera, investigate it. Remember, there is nothing that makes a shoplifter any different than an employee who steals; both parties have given in to a temptation and it is your job to stop it. This means that if you see an employee grab four copies of the same movie and start to walk off, watch them as you would a shoplifter. Make sure, however, that you are not seen doing this, as they will probably know what you are doing if they see you. If you suspect an employee is stealing merchandise from you and your cameras are not the best to pick it up on the sales floor, one of my favorite ways to catch them is a round robin. Have another loss prevention person from another store come over for a day and watch your employees. If the other loss prevention person acts just like a customer, your employees will have no idea that they are being watched. This typically works fantastic because most of the employees are on their best behavior when we are around, but when it's just customers, they can do what they want.

— **Integrity checks**: Oh, the debatable integrity checks that make some people cringe. There are many ways to do an integrity check, but you must first make sure that your company allows these to be done. It is a great controlled way to find a dishonest employee, and because of that, it is a very successful tool to use. Some companies do not like to put their employees in a situation where they have to choose to steal or not; however, they are in those same situations daily regardless. An integrity check is when you test the honesty of your employees to find out if they are going to steal or not when no one is looking. One of the easiest ways is to put some money on a gift card and then leave the gift card somewhere near the employee where they will find it. I used to load about $20 on a gift card and then drop it near an employee that I was going to check. I would go back on the cameras or watch from a safe distance to see what they would do next. Almost always, once the employee saw the gift card, they would look around to see if anyone was near. Once the coast was clear, they would scan the card to see how much money was on the card. After this, an honest employee would call a member of management to give it to them or place it in the lost and found. A dishonest employee, however, would pocket the gift card so that they could use it later. If they do pocket the gift card, the investigation has begun—but you must wait until they use the gift card. Normally, a dishonest employee will use it then or after their shift; if this happens, then you can stop them during the transaction and take them. They may decide to use it another day, and if that's the case then you need to know if you are going to stop them when they leave the store with the gift card or not. Another great integrity check, for stores that have their own credit cards, is a lost credit card payment. Use an envelope and put in about $40 cash with a bill for a store credit card and then drop it like you did the gift card. If the employee is honest, they will again take it to a member of management or process the payment for the customer; if they are not honest, then they will most likely throw away the envelope and bill while pocketing the money. This is a clear case of cash theft and can be handled right then.

— **Time alone**: When an employee is alone, it can have a big impact as to whether the employee will steal. Temptation alone is not going to have an employee steal; the employee must also feel as if they can get away with it. You can learn a lot about an employee when you watch them work by themselves, and I would encourage you to watch every employee work by themself at some point. An overnight stocker that works by himself knows that no one will see if he takes a drink without paying for it, so he may be more inclined to do so when the temptation arises. Try and find employees that work by themselves and spend a little bit of time watching them and seeing what they do—you might quickly find that some of them are paying their bills with your merchandise. Being alone gives them the opportunity to steal without being seen, so they may be more likely to steal.

— **Angry employee**: One of the leading reasons that employees start to steal is because they were mad at their manager or felt as though they got into trouble when they shouldn't have. When asking all of the employees that I have interviewed in the past why they started stealing, most often they would say that they were really pissed off at their direct supervisor and they felt they were owed something more. That's a big incentive to steal from your company, when you feel it owes you something, and you should watch employees that feel this way. I long ago started to ask store managers to let me know when an employee got into a lot of trouble, or felt as though their checks were shorted. I would then watch and see what the employee would do when they were away from everyone. A large amount of times, after the employee was upset and alone, they would break something in the store, damage the manager's vehicle, or steal merchandise to make up for what they were "owed." This does not mean that every employee who is upset will steal; however, it is a good time to watch an employee to see what they will do. If you have ever had an employee say that their check was shorted, it means they were expecting more and now need to figure out how to make up the difference. The best way to limit this from happening is to make sure the employee is calmed down before they leave the office after hearing the news that upsets them; an irrational employee is not going to be good at doing customer service anyway at the time; have them take a break if needed.

— **Personal items coming and going**: A personal bag has no place at a register that an employee is working, nor in a department where the employee will be. Every company should have some type of lockers set up for their employees to store their personal belongings while working, and this should be the only authorized place for their bags and belongings while on the clock. If you find an employee constantly bringing their purse to their register, even though they know the rules, there is probably something going on that needs your attention. Start to watch so that you can see why the employee needs their purse at the register; it could be quickly seen that they are using it to conceal merchandise or money that is not theirs. Many times I have seen employees bring their sweaters to a register although they would never wear them; after watching for a while, I have seen many of these sweaters used to conceal merchandise that the employee would steal after their shift was over. You can limit this type of theft from happening if you do not allow personal belongings anywhere other than their lockers, and enforce it.

— **Employee as customer**: Employees that watch shoplifters steal during their shift know exactly why those shoplifters got caught, and sometimes believe that they could have done better. Also, an employee might know that one of their friends is working on the register so they will be able to get a huge discount by going through their line. If you see one of your employees shopping while off the clock, it is not a bad idea to see what type of customer they are. Your employee knows better than the shopper what things they can get away with doing—make sure you are prepared for this and are watching to see what they do. If the employee checks out with one of their friends, it is a good idea to look at the transaction and see if they were given an unauthorized discount. This happens a lot because the cashier wants to take care of their friend so that they are taken care of next time. In this case, both employees are guilty of theft and should be handled according to your company's policy. Think of it this way: If the cashier gives an additional 20% off of a $100 transaction to their friend, your company just lost $20 that it should have received for the merchandise. This $20 loss is "shrink" and is prosecutable by most state laws for both employees.

— **Employee's family and friends**: This is very similar to an employee shopping off the clock. If you know that an employee's family members are shopping while the employee is working, watch and see what happens during the transaction. The employee could very easily give their friend or family a nice discount to help them out. In some occasions, the employee might not even scan every item when ringing up the transaction, letting the customer have some of the merchandise for free. If the employee wants to give a better discount than that, they may void out the transaction completely after their family has left; that way it will be like the credit card purchase never even happened. Keep a close eye when you know that a cashier is going to be in the situation to ring up someone they know; they may feel pressure to be dishonest for them.

— **Staged merchandise**: You should always be giving yourself time to walk around your store during the day; this should mean checking fitting rooms to make sure they are cleaned out, checking to make sure there are not empty packages in your stock rooms, and also looking out for merchandise that is placed somewhere irregular. If you go into the ladies' clothing stock room and find a small pile of electronics hiding, you should find that a little odd and begin to investigate. Start by seeing if you can find on camera which employee brought them into the stock room. Some employees know that they are the only ones that go into a particular stock room while they are on shift, so they feel safe storing the merchandise that they want in there. If they feel safe stashing the merchandise in the room, then you may want to make sure that they are planning to pay for the merchandise when they leave. It is typically against all company policies to let employees stash merchandise when it can be sold to the customer, but more importantly, if the merchandise is already out of sight it may be real easy for the employee to conceal the merchandise in their bag or a store bag and take it home without paying for it. If you find merchandise that looks to be staged like this, you should watch it to see what the employee is planning to do with it next.

Interrogations/ Employee Interviews

So you now have a dishonest employee that you need to interview but you don't know where to begin. There is a company out there that certifies loss prevention personnel so that they are proficient at conducting employee interviews. If your company doesn't mind footing the bill for this, then going to a Wicklander Zulawski seminar will help you when conducting interviews, but it can be a bit pricy if you are going to buy it yourself. A lot of companies send some of their loss prevention personnel to this class so that they can get a better interview rate and thus save the company more money; check with your company to see if this is an option for you. I will say that just because you have completed the class does not mean that you should do interviews, as I have seen many people that passed the course just to find out that they were no good under the pressure of conducting an interview. Just like the field of loss prevention, some people are meant to do it and some people are not. So if you have not taken the course and it is not an option for you, fear not, I am going to walk you through this and still give you the tools you need.

The first thing that you need to do is have the room ready for the interview. Having the room ready for an interview is crucial, even more so than having the room ready for a shoplifter. If you can, pick a room that doesn't already put the employee in a stressed mood, such as the loss prevention office. If an employee is going to the loss prevention office, they typically know what is going on and will quickly get tense. Although some store manager's offices are not much friendlier, it may be a little better than having them come to the "dungeon." Wherever you chose, make sure that there will not be any distractions, such as the phone ringing or people knocking on the door. Unplug the phone, hang a sign on the door, and make sure that there is no reason someone will need to come into the room during the interview. You do not want to be halfway through the interview just to have it interrupted by someone that makes the employee clam up again. Now that you have secured a room, make sure that there is nothing sharp or dangerous within reach of the employee; I have seen employees lose their head and do something silly once they knew they were caught. The seating of all three parties is also extremely important (you the interviewer, the employee, and a witness) and needs to be figured out before you bring the employee to the room. The employee should be seated closest to the door and facing into the office, this way it cannot come back later that you were blocking the employee in the room. The witness should be on the opposite side of the room and not directly facing the employee; you do not want the witness and the employee to be engaged in eye contact. You should be seated in the same type of chair as you have the employee in and only a few feet away from the employee; there should not be anything between you and the employee, like a desk, that would will cause a great mental separation between you two. If you are in the store manager's office, there is a temptation to use their chair and give the employee a crappy one, but this will start your interviewee off thinking that you are above them and not working together to find a solution. The same goes for having a desk between you; the desk symbolizes power and will instantly put the employee on guard. Have your chair and the employee's chair be of the same kind and facing each other with only about four feet between you, and you will find that they will have less of a guard up. Without the desk in between you two, you will also be able to mirror the employee when needed. When they cross their arms, or display another defensive stance because they do not want to talk with you, mirror their stance; make sure you are subtle and do not let them know what you are doing. After about three minutes, slowly release your defensive stance into a more relaxed sitting position. This will typically make the employee's subconscious also move to the same relaxed position because it is in sync with yours. If you are going to use this on your spouse, please do not let them know you learned it from here; my wife is still upset with me, thinking that I do this to her whenever she is upset. What can I say but old habits die hard?

The witness is an area of concern and must be methodically thought through when trying to decide whom to use. Either you or the witness must be of the same gender as the employee, to start. You do not want the witness to be a regular hourly employee because they will be more likely to tell others of what happened during the interview, and it will make the interviewee feel more embarrassed. You also want to try and make sure that your witness is not going to make the employee feel more stress or anxiety than they will already have; if the employee hates a certain manager, they are probably not the one you want to use as a witness. Your objective is to try and make the employee feel as relaxed as possible so that they are willing to talk with you; the last thing that will help you get information is an employee that feels like the witness is judging them. Once you pick your witness, they must follow one golden rule: do not talk during the interview, no matter what. I instruct my witnesses to not look at the interviewee or speak to them while I am interviewing them. If the witness engages in eye contact, then the employee might start to feel sympathy, anger, or any other emotion that I do not want them to feel at the time. Also, it will get the employee to focus more on the witness and not on me where I need it to make the employee feel as though I am the only one that can help them. The witness is also going to be very tempted to speak or ask a question, because they feel I might have missed something; however, there are certain questions that come at certain times, and having two people ask questions of a interviewee is a surefire way to make them tense up and stop talking. Make sure that your witness understands these rules and knows that their job is to just witness the interview. I like to have my witness scribble down notes throughout the interview with random time stamps—that way if I do need to go back to something, I can look it up in their notes. These notes can also be used if the case goes to court to further strengthen your side.

Once the room is ready, the witness has been prepped of the dos and don'ts, and you have some paper for the employee to write their statement on for later, it is time to get the employee. The following is the basic rudimentary script that I normally follow when conducting an interview. You do not want to be reading from a paper, but if you need to make yourself some bullet points to remember, just make sure they are out of sight of your interviewee. Also, do not take notes during the interview because this will make your employee feel as though they have to be careful about what they say and they will go quiet; if you need to remember something, you can always look at your witness's notes, but try to avoid this whenever possible.

(The witness is already seated in the back of the room and I am standing up, waiting for the employee to arrive in the office. The employee has been instructed to come to the office by another member of management and knock on the door. Once they knock, I open the door and instruct them to sit down at the chair that I have predesignated for them. For this scenario, I will be referring to the dishonest employee as Matt, because Mr. Employee gets old real fast.)

"Hello Matt, come in and have a seat here please. I am going to shut the door behind you to give us a little more privacy, but you are free to leave at any time that you wish." This is a crucial statement that you must say so that you cannot get into trouble for holding someone against their will before you charge them with something; in some courts this is called the "Freedom to Leave" speech.

"My name is Alan and I am the (title) for the company. I am conducting an investigation and recently your name has come up as one that I should speak with. I just have a few questions that I was hoping you could help me out with so that I can wrap this up. At the end, you and the company will both have some decisions to make to resolve the matters." This will undoubtedly get a puzzled look on your employees face: do not fear, they all do this.

"First, I want to explain exactly what loss prevention is and what we do. Loss prevention is the team that searches out where the company may be losing money, called shrink. Shrink happens in three main ways. First is when a customer comes into our store and takes something without paying for it. When they leave the store with the merchandise without paying for it, we consider them a shoplifter because they have caused the store a loss; we can no longer sell that movie they stole, and therefore lose money. The second way a store loses money is by paperwork errors. Imagine that you are working on the dock and it is your job to audit what we get from a truck delivery. If the paper says that we were billed for seven TVs but we only received six, we have a loss of one TV. If you were not paying attention and just marked off the sheet that we received the TVs, the store would have lost a few hundred dollars of shrink. The last one is employee theft (small pause); there are many ways that an employee can cause a company to lose money. An employee might do something similar to a shoplifter, such as taking merchandise without paying for it. An employee might take money out of the register and keep it for themselves; this is called till-tapping. An employee might give their friends an unauthorized discount at the register or may not even charge their friends for all of the items they were purchasing; this is called Sweethearting. An employee might hand out their discount card to their friends and family so that they can also get a discount at the store, even though the discount is only for the employee who works for the store." Whatever the violation is that you believe the employee to have committed, make sure to pause a little longer after you have said it and slightly nod your head while maintaining direct eye contact. This will put inside your employee's head that you already know what they have done.

"There are many ways that an employee can cause a loss to the store and it is my team's job to figure it out so that we can fix it and limit it from happening in the future."

"Now there are many tools that I am given to help me with finding and investigating all of the losses that happen within a store. First off, there is the paperwork. When I come to work in the morning, I am given a mound of reports about everything that has happened the day before, the week before, even the month and year before. These reports tell me everything from who was on a certain register that may have been short, to who gave a customer a large discount, to a certain credit card always going to the same cashier. See, everything that happens on a computer or register in this store is captured and sometimes flagged for me to review. Heck, if an employee does a No Sale, a report comes to me almost immediately so that I can look into it. Sometimes my investigations start from an anonymous tip. These tips can come from other employees that know of a violation being committed; sometimes it's even from people outside of the store that know of someone causing a loss from within the store. These people have been told firsthand of the violation and want to see it get resolved before the employee gets into severe trouble." This makes the employee further feel as though they have been caught, either by a report or by someone that told on them. Remember, most people have told a few friends of their violations.

"After the reports and the tips, I have my cameras. I am sure that you have seen the cameras around the store in the little dark domes, right? Those are the ones we want people to see and be aware of. See, there are three types of camera we use. The first is a still camera, which is normally placed above a register or somewhere that we want continuous observation. This camera is zoomed in so that we can see exactly what is going on at any given moment. These cameras do not move and are always on; they are very dependable when finding something that has caused a loss in a certain area. The next type of camera is called a PTZ, or pan-tilt-zoom camera. These cameras enable us to move them around in a complete 360° angle and even zoom in wherever we need them to. We can place one of them in the front of the store and zoom them in to see the other side of the store as if we were right there. They can even be zoomed in enough to read a credit card number from a register if needed. These come in very handy when there is a loss being caused that is just out of reach of our regular still cameras. The last type, however, is the best: our covert cameras. These cameras are the size of a tip of a pen and can be placed anywhere because they can be wireless. We may put them inside of a vent, smoke detector, inside of a register—anywhere that we may want to investigate further. This helps when we know that a loss is being caused in a certain place but we need a better picture of it. These three types of cameras are all hooked up to the DVR in my office. Unlike the DVR that you may have at home, mine records everything on every camera and can store it for a year or more. That means that, if I want to go back to a certain register a month ago and figure out why there was a no-sale done, or who opened up a package in the back store room, all I have to do is type in the day and begin watching." Try to insert what type of violation you believe that the employee has committed into this last sentence. This may make them a little more defensive, but it will again let them know that you already have your facts.

"Now here is where my job comes into play. With the reports, the tips, the cameras, the DVR, I can easily see exactly what happened *(pause)*; in fact, I can tell you the time it happened, where it happened, and even how it happened. If I wanted to, I could write up my report, put a little bow on it, and call it done *(pause)*, but that doesn't help either of us. See, I do not know the 'why,' and without this I cannot try and prevent it from happening in the future. If you see a spill on the floor, you may be tempted to wipe it up and call it a day. I, on the other hand, want to figure out why the spill got there so that we do not have the same problem happen in the future. Was the spill caused by a leaking bottle that is still on a shelf, was the spill caused from a hole in the roof that is going to continue to leak after we clean it? Without knowing why the spill is there, our job is not over. Now, rest assured I do not need to know why in order to finish my case; however, if I can understand why, I can sometimes help. By the time that I am at the point in my investigation where I am conducting interviews, I have spent countless hours doing research. That means that my report is full of pictures, reports, sometimes witness statements, and the reason that I do interviews is to allow me to hear your side of the story. Sometimes, by figuring out the why, we are able to come up with a solution together; but to do this, we have to be on the same page and work together with a good attitude.

"Let me tell you what I mean by a good attitude. The other night my buddy and I were going to meet some friends to hang out. My buddy was driving, and as usual, he was going a little over the speed limit. On this one road we were on, the speed limit quickly changed from 45 down to 30. Before my buddy slowed down to the proper speed, a police officer turned on his lights. See, what my buddy didn't know was that the police office was tasked to watch for speeders that come down that road. The police officer has been doing his job for years and is pretty good at being able to spot someone who is speeding. He uses his radar gun and waits patiently until his tool lets him know to go to work. By the time that the police were behind my buddy's car, he already knew that he was speeding; in fact, he knows what my buddy was doing, when he was doing it, how he was doing it, and soon who my buddy is. The only thing the officer does not know is why he was speeding. So my buddy pulls over and the police officer comes to the driver side door. He asks my buddy a very important question: 'Do you know why I pulled you over?' See, this question is so important because the officer wants to know if my buddy is going to have a good attitude or a bad attitude. If my buddy has a bad attitude, then the police officer will be less likely to help my buddy come up with a reasonable outcome. Obviously the officer already knows exactly what happened and just wants my buddy to be on the same page.

See, if the two are on the same page, they can then figure out what to do next. This does not mean that my buddy will not get a ticket; however, it stands to reason that he will be more likely to receive mercy from the officer by not trying to argue with him. Luckily, my buddy is a good guy and instantly admitted to his mistake. The police officer ran his information and ended up only giving my buddy a warning. This would not have been the case at all if my buddy started off the conversation telling the officer that he had no idea why he pulled him over.

"Matt, I am not a police officer. I do not wear a uniform, I do not have a blinking light above my car—but like the police officer, I am very good at what I do. Instead of a radar gun, I have reports, cameras, tips, and a very thorough investigation that is mostly wrapped up. The only thing that I do not know is why it happened. In the beginning I told you that you and the company will have some decisions to make, and this is where you have to decide to have a good attitude so that we may be able to work together to figure out a solution. So Matt, when was the first time you have caused a loss to the company?" The first person to speak loses; do not speak until they do. If you have gone over the interview with confidence to this point, then they are most likely going to tell you what they have stolen right now without hesitation. You have already planted the seeds that have made them believe you already know everything that they have done. Have tissues ready; if they start to tear up it is a sign of goodwill to be able to hand them one.

As the employee begins to say what they have done, your witness should be writing down everything that the employee admits to. Every time the employee admits to something else, try and get the employee to assign a reasonable dollar amount to it. If they say that they stole a movie, ask them how much they believe the movie is. This will help later on when trying to establish the dollar amount stolen. Also, try and have the employee give you an approximate date as to when they committed the violation.

Employee: "I stole a movie a few weeks ago. I know I shouldn't have done it, but I really wanted it."

You: "Was that the first time that you had stolen something from the store?"

Employee: "I'm not sure; I think I may have stolen about three movies total."

You: "About how much were these movies?"

Employee: "Probably about $20 each."

You: "How often do you steal in a week?"

Employee: "Only a couple of times a week."

You: "What kinds of things do you typically steal?"

Employee: "I don't know."

You: "Remember Matt, I have everything on camera. Right now I need you to be completely honest so that we can figure out how to handle this case. If I feel that you are not trying to be honest with me, then it does not show remorse for what you did and it does not help the company figure out what to do next for you."

Employee: "I think I have stolen maybe 6 movies, and 4-5 video games since I have been working here."

You: "When was the first time that you stole from the store?"

Employee: "The beginning of last month sometime."

You: "What caused you to want to steal?"

Employee: "I needed the money. I sold everything to the pawn shop down the road." (Now you know where the merchandise is and may be able to get it back. Also, the police will be able to pull a pawn record to see what was pawned that may be your merchandise.)

You: (This story will help when an employee is not truly considering how much they have stolen in the past from you. If you believe that the employee has stolen more than what they have said, especially when it comes to cash at the register, using this story will help them better understand what they have most likely done.) "When I was a kid, my dad had a large bowl of peanut M&Ms that he kept on the coffee table. No one was ever allowed to have any of the candy; it was just for him when he got off of work. One Friday, I remember my dad saying that he was going to leave for a fishing trip for the weekend; he again reminded me that the candy was to be untouched. I think I made it until Friday night until I had one of the M&Ms, and I think that was impressive because I loved peanut M&Ms. I remember a few more times that weekend that I snuck out to the coffee table and ate a small handful of M&Ms, but I never thought he would notice because the bowl was huge. Monday morning I woke up to my father yelling my name. I got out of bed and found him in the living room next to the coffee table. What was once a huge bowl overflowing with M&Ms was now completely empty. I had no idea that I had managed to eat all of the M&Ms over the course of the weekend, but a small handful at a time, I did. Now, I want you to really think about the movies that you have taken without paying for them. Why don't you start by telling me how many you would truly take during a week of work?"

Employee: "I think I would take about 5-6 a week."

You: "And you said you have been doing this since the beginning of last month, right?"

Employee: "Yes, about a week after I started."

You: "That was eight weeks ago, so if you have stolen about 5 ½ movies a week since then, you probably have stolen about 44 movies. Does that sound accurate?"

Employee: "Wow, I never added them up, but yeah, that sounds right."

You: "You said that they were about $20 each, too; so that would be about an $880 loss to the company, right?"

Employee: "Yeah, I'll pay it back though."

If you believe that there is other merchandise that the employee has stolen or if you believe that they have stolen cash, start to ask them about it now.

You: "What other things have you taken without paying for them here?"

I already know that the employee has admitted to stealing video games, but I want to get out all of the different types of items that he has stolen first. After I feel that I have all of the types of merchandise, I can then narrow down on each one to get how many of each and at what dollar amount. Giving them a chance to set the dollar amount for how much was taken will make it easier for them to fill out a statement later on admitting to the amount. Also, if the case does go to court, it was the employee that said they stole X amount and not you. They are the one that said how many movies a week, how many weeks, and what the dollar amount was; you just did the math for them.

Once the employee has further exhausted what they have stolen, how much, how many times, and you have agreed upon a dollar amount that the store has lost because of it, try and see what other information your employee will give you. "How did you learn to steal this way, was it another employee? Do you know of anyone else doing this type of theft? Do you know of anyone else stealing from the company?" Many times I am given names of other employees—but you have to consider your source and not jump to conclusions that the names given were in fact stealing. Asking who showed them how to do this type of theft does normally present a good lead to follow up with later, though. Once you have concluded the interview and feel as though you have all of the information, have the employee write a detailed statement about what they stole, how they did it, and how much they believe it to be valued at. Tell the employee that this is the time to give their side of the story, and let them know that the more details, the better. For a good air-tight statement, you really want the employee to admit what they stole, how they did it, and how much the total dollar amount was that they feel they cost the company; this statement will be the main piece of evidence if the case goes to court. In most cases, the dollar amount that the employee admits to on paper is how much the district attorney will charge them for stealing, even if you have a little bit of difference from your investigations. It makes it much easier to charge an employee for a dollar amount that they have already admitted to; there is no need to gamble on a case just for a few dollars more. So try and make sure that you both are in agreement of the total dollar amount lost before they write their statement.

From this point, it is up to your company and you to decide how you handle the employee. I will tell you that a lot of companies are big about prosecuting an employee, but you need to know what your district attorney is going to be looking for in order to try the case. The main thing that most district attorneys want is some type of evidence that a loss happened. Although the statement might admit to the theft of merchandise ranging from movies to video games, you may need some type of video or photographic proof of the theft. A picture of the employee leaving the store with a television matched with the employees statement that they stole a television that day is a slam dunk. However, if you had no idea about the merchandise before the interview and now have no way to print a picture of the crime, I would be very careful trying to prosecute the employee. Cash theft crimes can happen this way a lot, because you may know that a certain employee took the money since they are the only one on a register every time it is short so you conducted an interview; however, you lack any video evidence because the camera was out of focus or it was too hard to clearly see the theft happen. Accept the fact that you at least stopped one person from stealing for the time, and try to have them fill out a promissory note instead of prosecuting them. Most companies will do a promissory note instead of prosecuting an employee when they feel the conviction of the crime may be hard to get. Usually these promissory notes are handled much like a debt; the company continues to send the person bills until they pay off the balance that they have agreed to. Figure out exactly how strong your case is and then decide which option is better for you.

If you are having trouble making your employee admit that they have stolen before, relook at your introduction and make sure that it is strong and convincing. Your beginning is going to set the stage for the interview, so if you sound weak or unsure of yourself it will most likely make the suspect feel as if you are unsure if they truly stole or not. I have seen many interviews start off on the wrong foot because the interviewer did not sound confident and it made the suspect feel like they could deny everything.

Sometimes unexperienced interviewers do not know how to tell when their suspect is lying to them; if that is the case for you, this is going to be a big help for you going forward. At some point in the interview (probably after you get the first deny from your suspect), ask them something that they will have to remember back to, such as when they started with the company, who did their hiring interview, or what they had for breakfast last weekend. The question does not matter as long as they have to use their memory to think back to a certain situation. The answer is not important, but where their eyes go is greatly important; if the suspect's gaze goes up right or up left (these are the most common positions), then this is their control when they are trying to remember something truthful. Later on in the interview, if you ask a suspect a question and they then look opposite of their previous control gaze, they are most likely lying and accessing the creative side of their brain. The creative side of their brain will almost always be the exact opposite direction from when they are trying to remember something truthful. If you are really good, this is also the time to pick up on certain tells that the suspect has, like touching their face, scratching their elbow, or anything else that they do uncontrollably when they are telling a lie. Did I mention that I am always up for a game of poker if you have one going on?

Feel like a pro now, want to take on your first interview? I would suggest that you watch an interview first as a witness before you decide to take the reins. Once you feel comfortable being in the room and understanding the process, try doing a mock interview in the mirror a few times. This will make sure that you can easily get through the process without getting lost. Then, when you decide to conduct your first one, make sure that your witness is someone that is experienced with interviews so that they can rescue you if you get stuck. Don't worry about the jitters, they will never leave. Just like when you stop a shoplifter, your heart goes into your chest right beforehand; it still happens to me every time I say the line, "Tell me the first time you have caused the company a loss." I have conducted hundreds of interviews, yet that line is the moment of truth; the trick is to never let your employee see you sweat.

The more you can convey confidence, the more forthcoming the employee will be.

The Bar Stories

The following are some of the crazy stories that have happened to me and some of my fellow loss prevention acquaintances. If you are already in the loss prevention world, then these stories may just make you chuckle a little because you understand the insanity that can happen during a shift; however, if you are new to the loss prevention world, then these stories may open your eyes to the possibilities of what an experience can be like.

— **Spider Man Strikes Again**: So I decided to take a little time off from the loss prevention world and got a job running a video store for a while. After a couple of weeks at the store, I noticed that my sales were drastically down while one employee was working; I also noticed that a few dollars would be short from the safe on those same days. I decided to spend a night watching the employee, but knew that I couldn't let her see me in the store while I was there. After getting partial permission from my district manager, who had no idea what I typically do or how I do it, I decided to spend an evening doing surveillance. Since the employee would surely know that I was still in the building if I stayed anywhere in sight, I pretended to leave and parked my car a few blocks away. Once my vehicle was out of sight, I snuck back in and quietly went to the office. I knew that the employee would come to the office at some point and I didn't have a camera system hooked up, so I did the only logical thing I could think of and climbed into the rafters above the store. Because I knew that the rafter would be full of spiders, and I am terribly arachnophobic, I changed into my old Army fatigues before I came because they always make me feel more protected; besides, the extra pockets could hold some snacks for my long night. If I had planned my surveillance a little more, I would have found that the rafters only had a few beams that could have held my weight, but I didn't. Up in the rafters, I very slowly crawled across the beams to position myself above the register and opened one of the tiles so I could see below; I remember that journey across the store took almost an hour. Trying not to fall asleep, and going through nicotine withdrawals, I eventually saw the employee take a few dollars from the register and put them into her pocket. I promised my boss that I would not confront the employee without talking to him first, so I continued to wait. Later I also watched as she gave her friends a few brand new movies for free that would have normally cost about $25 each. I was pissed that I had to just watch as she continued to steal, and I debated spitting on her from above—after all, she would never know that it was I. At one point I leaned over the beam, seriously contemplating hocking a loogie onto her, and as I was in position to hit her, my hand slipped. My face and body came about an inch from hitting the tile and falling through to the floor below, but I somehow held my balance with my feet. The thought that I almost fell 20 feet worried me almost as much as blowing my cover; after all, how would you explain that you were in the rafters for almost two hours just watching someone? By the time her shift was over and I had officially hit past my muscle failure point, I crawled back above the office and watched as the employee took a few dollars from the safe and put them into her pocket. The thought of hocking a loogie didn't even cross my mind this time, because the fear of falling was still fresh in my mind. After the employee was done, she armed the store's alarm, took a brand new copy of the Spiderman movie without paying for it, and left the building. I must admit that I forgot about the alarm, but I always do most of my thinking on my feet. Both of my feet were asleep, my arms were too tired to hold me up any longer, and I knew that I only had 60 seconds to disarm the alarm before it would go off once it sensed my motion. The last thing that I wanted was to have the two police officers who worked for this small backwoods town come to my store in the middle of the night and question me as to what I was doing; they were already not fans of "outsiders" who did not grow up there. This was the type of town that seriously had no police on patrol after 10 p.m.;

instead, if there was an incident it would automatically call whomever's cell phone was on standby. So if I did set off the alarm, not only would the police have to respond to an "outsider" who looked like they were breaking into their own store, but they would also be half asleep and I am too pretty to go to jail, especially there. With 60 seconds before I would be held by someone who might tell me I have a "pretty mouth," all I could think about was WWSD—yep, what would Spiderman do? I moved a tile out of my way and decided I could swing down gracefully and without breaking my legs. As I dropped down to begin my swing, I was instantly reminded that my arms had already hit muscle failure and they decided not to hold my weight. Slipping from the beam while in mid-swing, I did a complete flip and miraculously landed on my feet. I impressed myself a great deal with still about 30 seconds left on the clock; I remember hearing spy music play in my head and feeling very accomplished. My excitement quickly left as I started to walk to the alarm system and saw my employee walking back into the store. The employee was frozen in place as she saw me, but at least someone was able to witness my amazing flip. The employee was speechless and I am not sure if it was because she was caught or because she had just witnessed the amazing Spiderman in real life; either way, she cried a little and gave back the money and movie. A few days later, shocked at what I had done for a stupid movie, my friends decided to call me Spiderman.

— **Just Stop Biting Me**: One of the worst things you can do in loss prevention is to let your guard down, but it's easy to do when you start to believe that you have seen it all. One day, while watching a teenage girl steal a few articles of clothing, I went to stop her as she went out the door. I didn't figure that the girl would give me much trouble, because she was a very small, nice looking girl. I should mention that this was the same day that I had a district audit at my store and so I had dressed up in a suit that I had just bought. In my new suit, which I could hardly afford, I approached the girl at the door and asked her to stop. The store itself was attached to a busy mall, and on this particular Saturday it seemed like the whole city was here to shop. The girl looked up at me a little puzzled and then smiled; I took her smile as a sign that she was going to be compliant and I pointed to the door. Her smile apparently was not that of compliance but that of an evil demon that had taken over her body and wanted nothing more than to make me pay for requesting her surrender. Smiling bigger, the girl began to yell as loudly as she could: "RAPE!" The parking lot was filled with shoppers leaving and coming into my store, and now all of them had their eyes on me. I was not about to let this evil smiling joker get away with my merchandise, so I decided to grab her arm as she yelled out. The yelling somehow got louder and now the crowds of people were drawing near me from all sides. One such customer was a little old lady with a cane who started to hit my leg and yell at me. I was not letting go of the girl no matter what, so as I had a good hold of her I looked at the old lady hitting me and tried to tell her what was going on. Talking to the old lady who did not seem to believe me, I felt a sharp pain on my arm that was holding the shoplifter. When I looked over, I saw that the shoplifter had my arm inside of her mouth, suit jacket and all. I am still not sure how the girl managed to dislocate her jaw enough to fit my arm inside of her fangs, but it didn't matter because it hurt like hell. Up until this point I had never had to hurt a female shoplifter, and I was not about to start, so all I could do was plead for my arm that was now dripping with blood. This was the first and only time that I remember being happy to see mall security pull up. Although I was embarrassed that they were needed to save my arm, I didn't care. The security guy saw the blood dripping from my suit and on to the ground, and he yelled out for me to hit the girl in the back of her head. Part of me thought that if I hit her she may bite down harder, part of me thought of a Rottweiler that would lock their jaw down, needing a crowbar to break the bite, and part of me still could not hit the girl. I finally told the girl that I would let her go free if she stopped biting me and she reluctantly let go of my arm.

She managed to run about two feet and then began to choke and gag from a mouth full of blood. She fell to the ground gasping for air, because she had swallowed and inhaled all of my blood. I didn't even try to help the girl in fear for my other arm, which still had a little bit of blood left in it. The police quickly drove up just as she collapsed to the ground, a pool of blood leaving her mouth. Scared to death, the police jumped out with their guns drawn on me; the sweet old lady called about a rape in progress and now the victim seemed to be lying unconscious. It didn't take long to fill the police in, but my brand new suit was ruined—all because I let down my guard. By the way, hepatitis shots are needed when someone bites you and they are not pleasant; my advice is to not let yourself get bitten.

— **Do You Have Time for an Interview**: While working at one store, I had an e-mail come across my desk about a man who had been stealing hundreds of dollars in jewelry from each of my neighboring stores. The man's picture seemed like a man whom I had just seen shopping in my own store, so I decided to go out and investigate what he was doing. I found the man in the clothing department, where he picked several items off the rack. Then the man went to the customer service department where he tried to return the merchandise, saying that he had just walked into the store with it. I nodded to the customer service lady to do the transaction so that I could stop the man once it was complete. The man instantly saw me and asked if I was a manager in the store; as the transaction was completed I told him that I was a manager, and in fact I was the manager of loss prevention. About to stop the man for the return theft, he instead interrupted me and asked me how he could get hired. I told him to fill out an application and someone would call him for an interview. He asked if I had time for an interview right now, so I smiled and said sure. My team was in place right behind him to stop him for the theft, but they started to laugh as they found out that he wanted an interview. The man followed me to my office, where I told him to have a seat; the rest of my team eagerly came into the office as well. I asked him why he would be good at loss prevention and he told me that he could spot a shoplifter easily. I said that I would need to role-play a little to see how well he would do, and he agreed. I asked him what he would say to someone that was stealing and was now caught, so he began to go into a long dialogue about what he would say. I then asked what he would say if the shoplifter was caught after stealing from multiple stores of mine and was looking at a felony charge. He again went into a long dialogue about what he would tell the shoplifter. I then asked what he would tell a shoplifter that was doing a return fraud in his store and then asked to be interviewed for a job. He began a new dialog of exactly what he would say, still not understanding that he was caught, or at least maybe hoping that he wasn't. So then I told him that I wanted to show him what the paperwork looked like and we could do a mock go at it. He agreed and we filled out the paperwork as we waited for the police to arrive. When the police came into the office, the man still seemed to be thinking that he was having a good interview. Sometime after the police put the man into handcuffs, he finally understood that this was not an actual interview. Before he left the room with the police, he asked, "When I get back, can we finish the interview? I really need the job."

— **I'm Just Really Well Endowed**: On one Black Friday while in a store, I decided to start my early morning off watching for potential shoplifters. As soon as the store opened, I saw two males walk into the store with their shoelaces untied and go to the shoe department. This being a telltale sign of a shoe thief, I was not surprised when both guys began to steal a pair of shoes each. One of the guys decided that he wanted a second pair as well, so he shoved the shoes down the front of his pants, where the shoes were still easily seen because of the huge shoe shape in his pants. I stopped the two guys at the door and asked them to come back with me, and one started to yell that he had not stolen anything. With a store full of Black Friday shoppers at 5 a.m., he began to scream,

"This man is stopping me because I'm just really well endowed." I couldn't help but to laugh, as the shoe was clearly pointing straight out at me from inside of his pants, but at least he had the nerve to try. I insisted that he take my shoes out of his pants before making any more of a scene and he complied. As he took them out of his pants he began to swing them around at me like they were nunchaku and threatened to start hitting people with them. The only thing funnier than a bad shoe thief hiding his stolen loot inside of his pants is a bad ninja who hits himself in the head with his own stolen shoes hard enough that he drops to the ground. Once on the ground, with a shoe print on his forehead, the guy gave up and came back to my office with his friend.

— **A Great Cart Pusher that Works for Free**: I came to work one day and noticed that there was a new employee bringing in carts from the parking lot. With over a hundred employees working at any given time, it was hard to know them all, but I thought I did. This employee was in proper dress code and was working hard, so I figured my team made a good choice hiring him, as he seemed to be good at his job. A few hours later, I received a call about a customer that was going to the back stock room and saying that he was an employee. It was the same new cart pusher that I had seen before. The other cart pushers on shift vouched for him that he was an employee, but something seemed odd. The new cart pusher was apparently helping out some customers that put some merchandise on hold in the back; he went to the back to get the merchandise for the customers and bring it to their car. I met up with him and told him that I would take care of it for him and to just keep up the good work with the carts. As I was telling him that I appreciated his hard work, someone radioed me in my earpiece that the cart pusher was a fake and not a real employee. I started to laugh uncontrollably because of the amazing façade that he had played. I asked if he would come to my office to talk about his growth potential and he agreed. While in my office, I let him know that I knew he wasn't an employee, and he said, "Well I could be if you hired me." Meanwhile the two "customers" that were waiting for him to bring them their merchandise were apprehended for stealing. Apparently the three were all working together to steal merchandise, but never ended up getting a chance to steal anything. The fake cart pusher had worked almost a full shift without stealing a thing, but my parking lot was crystal clear of carts. I ended up not charging the guy with anything and thanked him for his horrible shoplifting skills; I even let him know that he was invited to push my carts again if he was bored.

— **You Hit Like a Girl, a Really, Really Big Girl**: Sometimes when working in loss prevention you think you are invincible, so when you are going to stop two female shoplifters you don't normally hesitate even if their combined weight is 750 lbs. and you are not even 200 lbs. Watching on camera, I saw two ladies begin to steal children's clothing; they ripped off the hangers and shoved the merchandise into their pants and shirts. After about 15 minutes of collecting merchandise, the two ladies started to leave the store and walked to the front doors. I anxiously walked outside to head them off and met them as they tried to walk outside. I remember smiling as I announced who I was, thinking that they would easily comply and come back to the office with me. As soon as I spoke, one of the ladies took a swing at me, nearly making herself fall to the ground. I was a little shocked, because I hadn't planned for them to become violent, so I turned my attention to the other lady and asked her to stop. Again as I spoke, the second lady also took a swing at me and missed. So I decided that I would just stand in front of them, because it wasn't like they could move me—I was wrong. It was if I were trying to stop a very slow-moving train from leaving the station, all aboard or all get run over. I fell down quickly and was a little embarrassed, so I decided to try again. The second and third times that I walked in front of them, I had the same outcome: failure. No more mister nice guy I thought, so I decided to take one of them by the arm and put them in an arm bar. In my head it seemed like a much easier idea, but I had yet to do an arm bar on anyone quite as big as these ladies. To get enough force, I practically had to grab their arm and swing like I was Tarzan to the other side. A few swings and finally I had the momentum; Godzilla came crashing down to the ground. Looking at the surveillance video later, I apparently bounced on top of the female a few times as we hit the ground. After all of that work, I was not about to let go of my prized possession to try and stop the other female, so I figured one was good enough. I felt liquid coming from the top of my head, and it wasn't until the liquid hit my face that I felt the pain coming from the back of my head; the other shoplifter was punching me in the back of the head with some spiked ring, causing my head to nearly crack in half. I told her I was not letting go of her friend so she may as well come back with me. Just then, one of my more experienced female employees came out and told the shoplifters that she knew karate so they better leave; the look on this grey-haired employee's face meant business. With most of my employees outside now, it seemed crazy that the eldest was the one willing to get into a bar fight to have my back, but it was still appreciated. The second lady stopped hitting me, as I continued to wrestle her friend like an alligator, and jumped into their car, which was right in front of us in the parking lot. The lady searched the car for something and then finally came back to let me know she was going to run me over. I found out later that the females had a gun in the car but it wasn't in the spot that they usually kept it; if she would have looked under the passenger's seat I would not be here today. The car started and I could hear the engine rev. I might have jumped off, but I had already spent so much effort and blood on this one that I didn't want to let go. The car drove into me just enough to give me a bump on the head, and then it drove away like hell, leaving the alligator on her own. The police came and ended up getting both ladies. The driver ended up pulling a gun on one of the cops and it caused her to get a few new piercings, but she still managed to stay alive. It came out that the females were on the run from multiple warrants but no one was able to stop them before, or dumb enough to try. I began to reconsider my life choices that night as I iced every part of my body, but the next day I received two different letters of praise from both the police chief and the city, so I decided I was right where I should be, if just a little bruised.

— **My New Best Friend**: Sitting in my office, trying to get some paperwork done that the company decided loss prevention managers should do daily instead of real work, I received a phone call about a disturbance in one of our kiosk stores. Inside of my store, we rented out space to a fast food business that was serving breakfast at the time of the call. When I walked up to the store, I noticed that all of the customers were against the wall to my left, and all of the employees were in the back of their kitchen to the right; in the middle was my new friend, whom we will call "Ali." Ali was a rather large man with the build of a heavyweight boxer, and all he wanted was a breakfast sandwich; the problem was that his bank card did not have enough money to pay for the sandwich. As I walked up to him, he was yelling, "Someone give me my F'ing sandwich before I kill you all." In my head I wondered why the store didn't just give him a sandwich so he could be on his way, but I wasn't paid to make great decisions like that; no, today I was employed to be Ali's sparring partner. As I walked up, I quickly decided that I would just buy Ali his much-needed egg nutrients and call it a day. I called over to one of the employees and told him that the sandwich was on me; they stayed ducked down behind the counter as they handed me the sandwich. I asked Ali if we could take a walk outside as he ate so I could get to know him more. His reply was, "Sure we can go outside, but you know I have to kill you." Well, at least I could get him away from close quarters with a lot of customers before I go. While we walked, Ali continued to tell me that I was the nicest guy that he had ever had to kill, and he sure did appreciate the sandwich that I bought him. The man spoke in an almost-drunk voice, but there was no smell of alcohol or any other drugs that I could detect. I started to debate whether I was going to try and fight Ali, since he had to be much slower than me, or if I was just going to play possum once he took the first punch—if I survived it. As soon as we got outside, Ali was finishing the last bite of my final meal; I don't think he got the memo that the person about to die was supposed to be the one that ate. He threw the trash away and said, "All right, it's time to kill you." I figured I could just buy a little more time with Ali and wait for the police to show up; that is, as long as someone had called the police by now. I couldn't think of what to talk about, so I just ignored the threats and asked Ali what kind of hobbies he liked. I ran down a list of different hobbies and he quickly stopped me and said no to each one. He pulled back his fist as to take his first punch, while I clenched and braced for the impact, and then he said "I like video games." The voice that came out of Ali was all of a sudden very different than the voice that wanted to kill me; this voice was much like a child's about the age of five. Adapting is a great survival skill that has got me through the Army, security, marriage, and now Ali. I asked what types of games he liked to play, and he again seemed to be in the mind frame of a five-year-old, rocking back on his heels and grinning as he told me that he played a game called *Injustice*. "I play as Superman and I fly really, really, high." I began talking to him about the game and asking questions that he seemed to enjoy answering. I asked once if he thought I would be any good at it, and he said back in his drunken-boxer voice, "No, I would destroy you!" Fair enough, competition is not what you should try and start with a guy that just wanted to kill you; so I went back to asking him as many details about the game as possible. As he was talking to me about the game in a voice that reminded me of my own boys at home, the police pulled up and walked behind him to handcuff him. He didn't seem to even notice that they were there until the last cuff was put on. Once the last click happened, Ali began to rage up again and threated to kill us all. The police jumped back and pulled out their guns. Feeling like I had a knack for calming this guy down, I started back at the conversation with Ali as I walked him to one of the squad cars and coaxed him into the seat. I told him I was going to get in on the other side so he continued to tell me about the game as we shut the door. Once he noticed that I was not coming with him, he began to yell and rock the police cruiser from side to side in a way that I was sure would flip the car over. Apparently Ali had a few medical problems and had escaped his care earlier that morning. I was so relieved when he drove off in the back of the cruiser, hoping that I would never see him again. Three months later he was back in the store with an ice cream cone in hand. I tried to stay away from him, but kept an eye on him from afar. He spotted me from across the way and began to yell my name as he ran toward me. As a giant would leap over trees to catch his prey, Ali began to leap over everything in his path between he and I. I didn't know what to expect from Ali, so again I braced for anything. Once he reached me, Ali picked me up high and began to hug me like I was his long-lost teddy bear that he had misplaced. "Alan, I have missed you so much. I was afraid I would never see you again." At least he was in a good mood and the little boy voice was present, but as he put me back down, he said in his drunken-boxer voice, "You're my best friend, and it's not very nice to put your best friend in jail. Why did you put me in jail, Alan?" Quickly I brought up the video game again and Ali was as happy as ever. He skipped off and left the store while I promised to come visit him sometime and watch him play. I have yet to play that game with my boys in fear that Ali will randomly show up at my doorstep demanding that I play with him instead.

— **That's Not Merchandise, That's My Baby**: One afternoon, I watched as a young girl began to select dozens of bottles of perfume. She then put the bottles into her shirt, which slowly began to inflate. This was the first time that I had seen an inflated theft tool being used by a shoplifter, but I had heard about them before. The contraption was meant to make the suspect look as if they were pregnant, and it was pretty convincing. The girl left the store after a few dozen bottles and I attempted to stop her. She instantly claimed that she was pregnant and going into labor so I was not to touch her. I knew of course that she was not pregnant, but that didn't stop my customers coming into the store from thinking that I was picking on a pregnant lady. I didn't want to grab the girl because she was making a large scene, so I just kept getting in her way when she tried to leave. She called 911 on her cell phone and told the operator that she was going into labor but some man was trying to kidnap her; the police showed up in record time. The first officer on scene was a good friend of mine, so I told him what was going on and he put his attention on her. He asked to see the merchandise and she began to scream like she was really in labor. Her acting was so good that I almost doubted what I had seen before. The officer walked closer to her and was about to place his hand on her shoulder to calm her down when she kicked him in the crotch as hard as she could. The officer, about 6′ 6″, quickly went to the ground and to his knees in pain. I grabbed the girl as she tried to run just as the officer slipped out his Taser and pulled the trigger at the girl. The Taser hit us both and we began to synchronize-shake like it was an Olympic event. Perfume bottles went crashing down from her shirt all around us as we both fell to the ground. I kind of wish that the glass from the bottles was the problem, but it was the combined smell that really choked me up. I must have taken ten showers before the smell finally left my skin.

There are hundreds of other stories that I could tell you about my past experiences, and I have learned something new from every one I have been lucky enough to walk away from. I have had multiple guns, knives, nunchaku, and swords pulled on me over the years, but I believe the most successful times were when I could find a way to talk the person down from hurting either one of us. Your first option should not be to try and subdue your attacker by defensive maneuvers, but to disarm your attacker by engaging in the problem. Being in loss prevention, you are not normally equipped with a bulletproof vest or any other type of protection, although sometimes you may need it; the best thing you have is your quick thinking and sometimes a little luck. If you can have a shoplifter drop his gun while it is pointed at you from a few feet away, you should consider yourself a hero in his eyes and your family's eyes. No one should have to end their life over a stolen copy of *Night at the Roxbury*, so try and resolve the issue without the use of force, or the least amount possible.

While in loss prevention, you are going to become a little jaded and start to believe that everyone around you is a thief and that it is up to you to prove it. While this may be a good way to find internals, it is not the way to live your own personal life. I have spent years trying to find the switch that will let me be the normal person once I leave my store; I am sure that prison guards, police, and other similar jobs require the same. If you are going to continue or start in loss prevention, remember that going home is the most important part of your day, both for you and your shoplifter; if you can really get behind this concept, then you should be able to keep control of that switch that lets you relax once your schedule permits. I hope you find things in this book to make you more productive at preventing shrink in your stores, and also that help open your eyes to some other possibilities that could happen along the way if you are not careful. I'm going to leave you with one last story of mine that I hope will really make you think every time you are in a similar situation.

I had just been promoted from my store, so a new manager was slated to take my old position. After a few weeks of training, he was out on his own and doing great. He spotted a suspect loading up a cart full of electronics that he believed would be stolen, so he waited by the door. The suspect ran out a fire escape and into the parking lot where he had a van waiting for him. At this company, we had no boundaries of where we could go to chase down a shoplifter, so my buddy chased him to his van. Once at the van, the shoplifter jumped inside the passenger door and left the cart of merchandise. My buddy ran to the side of the van where the merchandise was, and the side door of the van opened up. From inside the van, three guys jumped out and dragged my buddy into the vehicle. About five miles down a busy highway, they threw my friend out, half-dead. He spent many weeks in critical condition before he was released. You can say that my buddy didn't keep watch of his surroundings, or that he shouldn't have done a stop in the parking lot because they are dangerous, or anything else that you want—the point is to remember that the most important part of your day is going home safely.

Illustrations

Mock Report

Your company probably has a certain way that they like their reports to be written; if so, give yourself a good template so that you can just fill in some blank spaces in order to save yourself time. If you do not have any report writing experience, this one should help you cover all of the basics of a good report. (Remember that normal grammar is not key here; this format is what is used for cases in most court systems. There will be run-on sentences and other things that might make you cringe if you are an English major.)

On 2/17/2015, I, Alan Hoekman, Loss Prevention District Manager for Store Name, watched as an unknown male, later identified as John Smith, walked into the shoe department. Smith was wearing a black pair of sneakers when he walked into the department with his shoelaces untied at approximately 1310. At approximately 1312, Smith grabbed a box of white shoes from the display and carried them out of the department. Smith walked with the shoes toward the back of the store while I maintained continuous observation of Smith and the shoes. At approximately 1315, Smith walked into the toy department, where he took his black shoes off and put on the white shoes that were inside of the box. Once the unpaid-for white shoes were on Smith's feet, Smith placed the black shoes in the box and placed the box on a rack inside of the toy department. Smith then walked out of the toy department, still wearing the unpaid-for merchandise on his feet, and began to walk to the front of the store. At approximately 1318, Smith walked past the last registers without paying for the merchandise, and continued to walk to the front door. At 1319, Smith walked through the first set of doors toward the parking lot. While maintaining continuous observation of Smith and the shoes, I approached Smith in the vestibule and identified myself as loss prevention. I led Smith back to the loss prevention office, where we arrived at 1320. Once inside the office, I asked Smith for the unpaid-for merchandise. Smith then handed me the pair of shoes that he had taken. I asked Smith why he had taken the shoes and he said that he was planning to sell them to a friend. When I ran Smith's SSN in the company's database, I found that Smith had been stopped twice before and had been issued a trespass for his past thefts. I gave Smith a copy of the Civil Demand notice and had Smith sign a new Trespass agreement. I informed Smith that this Trespass agreement was for life, and he could not come back to any of our company's stores. Police were contacted at 1340 and arrived at 1410, at which point they took Smith into custody; Officer Atler (badge number #1234) was the first responding officer. Smith's court date is scheduled for 3/12/2015. Total Case Value before tax: $59.99.

Known Theft Board

A known theft board is a great tool in helping you get your whole store to engage with the loss prevention team and at the same time helping your loss prevention team find where your merchandise is being stolen. If you place this board in the back of your store someplace where all of your employees can get to it easily, you will see them all start taking an active step in helping your store prevent shrink. If you can find a premade map of your store, that will be best; if not, you can make one using Microsoft Word. The first image is of a Microsoft Word map without pins and the second is what it will look like with a few pins in it.

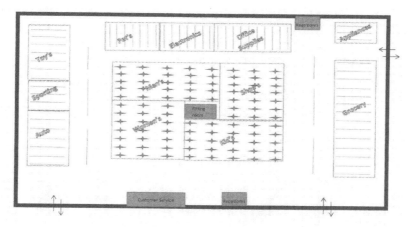

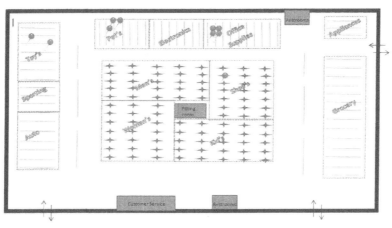

While writing this book, I was sent a picture of my Known Theft Board being used at a store that I have never been to and from a company that I no longer work at. I sent directions on how to do this map to a few districts to get them on the right track just before I left, and it seems as though they are doing it great. Apparently for this store, their whole district is required to do it now because of the results that they have had from it. Look carefully at the pins on the map and see where their theft trends are.

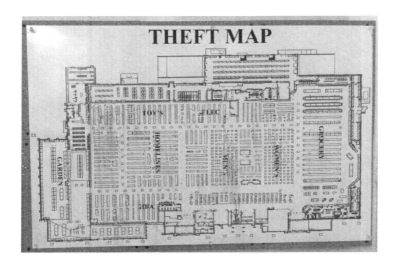

Employee Recognition Board

This is a tool that will help get employees excited about helping out the loss prevention team by giving them vocal credit or even a small monetary gift. I have used this in many companies across many stores, and have always seen a significant increase in engagement and great return on investment. The following is a basic template that I normally use. If an employee (or team) saves the store $100,000, then you will end up paying them $440 in gift cards, two sodas, and a candy bar; I'm pretty sure any store manager out there will go for it, but you can always adjust to meet your store demands.

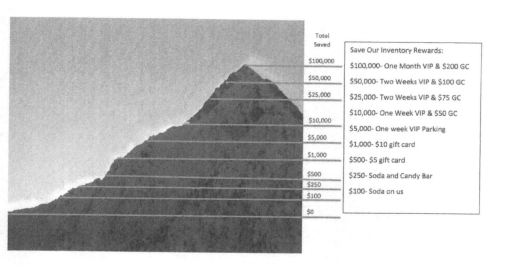

Total Saved

$100,000
$50,000
$25,000
$10,000
$5,000
$1,000
$500
$250
$100
$0

Save Our Inventory Rewards:

$100,000- One Month VIP & $200 GC

$50,000- Two Weeks VIP & $100 GC

$25,000- Two Weeks VIP & $75 GC

$10,000- One Week VIP & $50 GC

$5,000- One week VIP Parking

$1,000- $10 gift card

$500- $5 gift card

$250- Soda and Candy Bar

$100- Soda on us

Over/Short Tracker

This system will help keep track of employees that continue to be on a register that is short. This report will not automatically tell you that you have a dishonest employee, but if the same employee is on the register every time it's short, there is probably a reason for it. Using this report and working alongside the person who does the financials for your store is a great way to get on top of your till-tapping theft. After you set up the system, it should take you no more than a few minutes a day to input the numbers into the system and quickly guide you to an employee of interest.

	#1	#2	#3	#4	#5	#6	#7	#8	#9	#10	#11	#12	#13	#14	#15
1-Jan	-10														
2-Jan															
3-Jan	10	-10										-10			
4-Jan		10													
5-Jan	-10											-10			
6-Jan			10												
7-Jan										25					
8-Jan	-10		-10		5					-25		10			
9-Jan	-10														
10-Jan				-5											
11-Jan															
12-Jan	-10														
13-Jan													10		
14-Jan															
15-Jan	-10												-10		
16-Jan					-5										
17-Jan															
18-Jan	10														
19-Jan															
20-Jan															
21-Jan															
22-Jan															
23-Jan															
24-Jan															
25-Jan															
26-Jan															
27-Jan															
28-Jan															
29-Jan															
30-Jan															
31-Jan															

This first screenshot shows you how to set up the Day/Register page. You can put in an Excel rule to make any register turn red after more than three days short within a month. Sometimes the short is just an error and will be corrected the next day; in this case, highlight it yellow so you do not waste time trying to figure out who stole money on those days.

	#105	#107	#209	#212	#218	#225	#285	#291	#253	#299	#301	#323	#325
	0	3	2	0	2	2	2	2	2	2	2	2	2
1-Jan	X			X			X				X		X
2-Jan													
3-Jan	X	X	X	X			X		X		X		x
4-Jan													
5-Jan	X		X		X				X		X	X	
6-Jan													
7-Jan													
8-Jan	X	X		X	X			X		X			
9-Jan	X					X		X					
10-Jan												X	
11-Jan													
12-Jan	X												
13-Jan													
14-Jan													
15-Jan	X	X											
16-Jan													
17-Jan													
18-Jan	X					X							
19-Jan													
20-Jan													
21-Jan													
22-Jan													
23-Jan													
24-Jan													
25-Jan													
26-Jan													
27-Jan													
28-Jan													
29-Jan													
30-Jan													
31-Jan													

This next screenshot shows you how to have the Day/Employee page set up. You can put in an Excel rule to turn any employee red that has shown up on this report more than three days in a month (you can also make one that turns another color if the employee is on it nine times within the last three months). Looking at this report, you can see clearly that employee #105 needs to be watched because they are on the most amount of registers that are coming up short.

Shoplifter Survey

If you use this survey while you are processing your shoplifter, you will uncover information about the shoplifting that is taking place in your store. Not every shoplifter will give you information or even the truth; however, sometimes you will learn about a group that is stealing from you or that is buying your stolen merchandise this month. If you are spending time playing on your phone while waiting for the police to show up, you may as well try to get some information out of your shoplifter. This report can also be used against the shoplifter in court, so make sure to give a copy of it to the district attorney if there is valid, usable information on it. While the questions may seem silly, when they are answered by the shoplifter and filled out by themselves, they have a hard time disputing what they wrote when they go to court.

Name: _____

Date: _____

Why are you here today? _____

Have you done this before? _____

How many times a month/week do you do this? _____

What other stores do you do this at? _____

Why do you feel comfortable doing it here? _____

What do you normally do with the merchandise afterwards? _____

   If you sell it, where? _____

Who do you know that works at this store? _____

Did they help you today or before? _____

Do you plan to do this again? _____

Employee Interview Room Sketch

All rooms are going to be different when you do an employee interview; however, there are a few points to remember for every interview when preparing your room. Also, including a drawing of the room may help in some cases that go to court to make sure that the suspect did not feel trapped inside of the room.

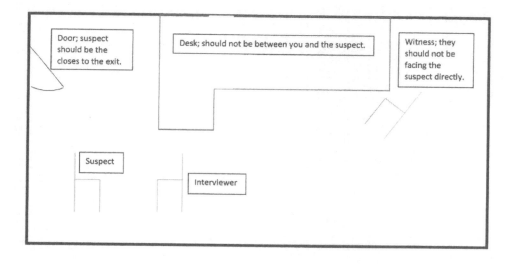

Employee Interview Flow Chart

While every interview is going to have its differences, having a certain flow that you typically follow is going to improve your speech and in turn your prosecution rate. Make changes to the flow as you see fit or to adjust for your type of employee theft, but keeping a solid beginning is crucial in helping convey your knowledge of their crime.

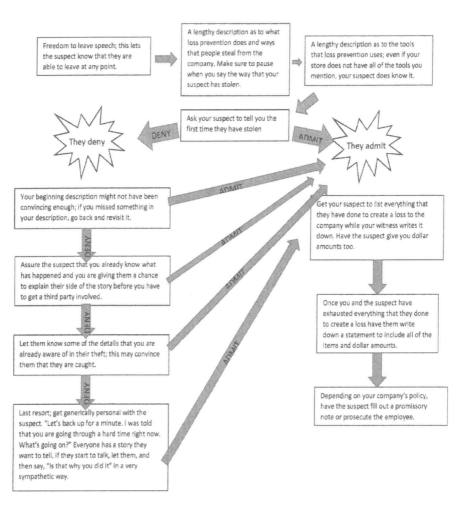

Made in the USA
San Bernardino, CA
28 March 2015